@Copyright 2020by Monique Hardy- All rights reserved.

This document is geared towards providing exact and reliable information in regards to the topic and issue covered. The publication is sold with the idea that the publisher is not required to render accounting, officially permitted, or otherwise, qualified services. If advice is necessary, legal or professional, a practiced individual in the profession should be ordered.

Under no circumstance will any legal responsibility or blame be held against the publisher for any reparation, damages, or monetary loss due to the information herein, either directly or indirectly.

Legal Notice:

The book is copyright protected. This is only for personal use. You cannot amend, distribute, sell, use, quote or paraphrase any part or the content within this book without the consent of the author.

Disclaimer Notice:

Please note the information contained within this document is for educational and entertainment purposes only. Every attempt has been made to provide accurate, up to date and reliable complete information. No warranties of any kind are expressed or implied. Readers acknowledge that the author is not engaging in the rendering of legal, financial, medical or professional advice. The content of this book has been derived from various sources. Please consult a licensed professional before attempting any techniques outlined in this book.

CONTENTS

- Cuisinart Air Fryer Oven overview 6
  - AIRFRYERCHART 6
  - BEFOREFIRSTUSE 8
  - OPERATION 10
  - CLEANING AND MAINTENANCE 13
- Breakfast and Brunch Recipes 14
  - Eggs with Turkey & Spinach 14
  - Eggs with Ham & Veggies 14
  - Eggs in Bread & Tomato Cups 15
  - Eggs in Bread & Sausage Cups 16
  - Eggs in Bread & Bacon Cups 17
  - Spinach & Mozzarella Muffins 18
  - Bacon & Spinach Muffins 19
  - Ham Muffins 19
  - Savory Carrot Muffins 20
  - Potato & Bell Pepper Hash 22
  - Apple Fritter Loaf 23
  - Enchiladas 4 Breakfast 24
  - Cinnamon Streusel Bread 25
  - Brioche Breakfast Pudding 26
  - Strawberry Basil Muffins 27
- Poultry Recipes 29
  - Roasted Goose 29
  - Christmas Roast Goose 29
  - Chicken Kebabs 30
  - Asian Chicken Kebabs 31
  - Kebab Tavuk Sheesh 32
  - Chicken Mushroom Kebab 32
  - Chicken Fajita Skewers 33
  - Zucchini Chicken Kebabs 34
  - Chicken Soy Skewers 35
  - Chicken Alfredo Bake 35
  - Buffalo Chicken Tenders 36
  - Turkey Turnovers 37
  - Chicken Parm 38
  - Teriyaki Duck Legs 39

  Turkey Burgers 40

Vegetables Recipes 41

  Glazed Veggies 41

  Parmesan Mixed Veggies 41

  Veggie Kabobs 42

  Beans & Veggie Burgers 43

  Marinated Tofu 44

  Crusted Tofu 45

  Tofu with Orange Sauce 46

  Tofu with Capers 47

  Tofu in Sweet & Sour Sauce 48

  Tofu with Cauliflower 49

  Spaghetti Squash Lasagna 50

  Green Chili Taquitos 51

  Chickpea Fritters 52

  Roasted Fall Veggies 52

  Asian Tofu "Meatballs" 53

Fish and Seafood Recipes 55

  Shrimp in Lemon Sauce 55

  Garlic Shrimp Skewers 55

  Shrimp Skewers with Pineapple 56

  Teriyaki Shrimp Skewer 57

  Cajun Shrimp Skewers 58

  Italian Shrimp Skewers 58

  Prawn Burgers 59

  Bang Bang Breaded Shrimp 60

  Taco Fried Shrimp 61

  Garlic Mussels 61

  Mussels with Saffron Sauce 62

  Cajun Shrimp Bake 62

  Shrimp with Garlic Sauce 64

  Shrimp Scampi 54

  Shrimp Parmesan Bake 65

  Shrimp in Lemon Sauce 66

  Garlic Shrimp Skewers 66

  Shrimp Skewers with Pineapple 67

  Teriyaki Shrimp Skewer 68

Cajun Shrimp Skewers	69
Italian Shrimp Skewers	69
Prawn Burgers	70

Beef, Lamb & Pork ... 72

Pork with Quinoa Salad	72
Pork Garlic Skewers	73
Zesty Pork Skewers	73
Alepo Pork Kebobs	74
Zucchini Pork Kebobs	75
Lime Glazed Pork Kebobs	76
Pork Kebab Tacos	77
Rainbow Pork Skewers	77
Tangy Pork Sausages	78
Roasted Pork Shoulder	79
Salmon Burgers	80
Air Fried Haddock Filets	80
Crispy Coated Scallops	81
Tasty Tuna Loaf	82
Maryland Crab Cakes	82
Mediterranean Sole	83
Coconut Shrimp	84
Spicy Grilled Halibut	85
Tropical Shrimp Skewers	85
Seafood Mac n Cheese	86

Snacks & Appetizers ... 88

Cheddar Biscuits	88
Lemon Biscuits	88
Potato Bread Rolls	89
Veggie Spring Rolls	91
Spinach Rolls	92
Cheese Pastries	93
Veggie Pastries	94
Spinach Dip	95
Chili Dip	96
Onion Dip	96
Crispy Sausage Bites	97
Puffed Asparagus Spears	98

- Wonton Poppers 99
- Party Pull Apart 99
- Easy Cheesy Stuffed Mushrooms 100

Dessert Recipes 101
- Quick Coffee Cake 101
- Gluten-Free Fried Bananas 101
- Vanilla Almond Cookies 102
- Lobster Tails with White Wine Sauce 102
- Broiled Lobster Tails 103
- Paprika Lobster Tail 104
- Lobster Tails with Lemon Butter 104
- Sheet Pan Seafood bake 105

CUISINART AIR FRYER OVEN OVERVIEW

AIRFRYER CHART

The chart below lists recommended cooking times, temperatures, and portions for various types of foods that can be Airfried in the Cuisinart AirFryer Toaster Oven.

If portions exceed recommendations, you can toss occasionally while cooking to ensure the crispiest, most even results. Smaller amounts of food may require less time. For best airfry results, use the oven light to periodically check on food.

Food	Recommended Amount	Temperature	Time
Bacon	8 slices	400°F	8 to 10 minutes
Chicken Wings	3 pounds, about 20 wings	400°F	20 to 25 minutes
Frozen Appetizers, (e.g., mozzarella sticks, popcorn shrimp, etc.)	1 1/2 pounds, about 28 frozen mozzarella sticks	400°F	5 to 7 minutes
Frozen Chicken Nuggets	1 pound, about 34 frozen chicken nuggets	400°F	10 minutes
Frozen Fish Sticks	12 ounces, about 20 frozen fish sticks	400°F	8 minutes
Frozen Fries	1 to 2 pounds	450°F	15 to 25 minutes
Frozen Steak Fries	1 to 2 pounds	450°F	15 to 25 minutes
Hand-Cut Fries	2 pounds, about 3 medium potatoes, cut into 1/4-inch thick pieces, about 4 inches long	400°F	15 to 20 minutes
Hand-Cut Steak Fries	2 pounds, about 3 medium-large potatoes, cut into eighths lengthwise	400°F	15 to 20 minutes
Shrimp	1 pound, about 16 extra-large shrimp	375°F	8 to 10 minutes

| Tortilla Chips | 6, 5-inch tortillas cut into fourths | 400°F | 5 to 6 minutes, toss halfway |

Airfrying doesn't require oil, but a light spray can enhance browning and crispness. Use an oil sprayer to keep it extra light, or pour a little oil into a bowl, add food, and toss.

BEFORE FIRST USE

Place your AirFryer Toaster Oven on a flat surface.

Before using, move oven 2 to 4 inches away from the wall or from any objects on the countertop. Do not use on heat-sensitive surfaces.

OBJECTS SHOULD NOT BE STORED ON THE TOP OF THE OVEN. IF THEY ARE, REMOVE ALL OBJECTS BEFORE YOU TURN ON YOUR OVEN. THE EXTERIOR WALLS GET VERY HOT WHEN IN USE. KEEP OUT OF REACH OF CHILDREN.

GENERAL GUIDELINES

AirFry: This function is used to AirFry meals as a healthy alternative to deep frying in oil. The AirFry function uses a combination of hot air, high fan speed and 4 upper heating elements to prepare a variety of meals that are both delicious and healthier than traditional frying.

Use the provided Baking Pan and AirFryer Basket when using the AirFry function. Place the AirFryer Basket onto the Baking Pan. Use Rack Position 2 for AirFrying.

Bake: Baking is recommended for a variety of foods you would normally prepare in your conventional oven. Baked goods that require a more gentle cooking method like cakes, muffins and pastry yield best results on Bake. Convection Bake uses a fan to circulate heated air around food to cook faster and is ideal for even browning. It is best used for heartier baked goods such as scones and bread and is also excellent for roasts, poultry, pizza and vegetables.

Use the Baking Pan for fresh pizza (in Rack Position 1) and the rack alone if pizza is frozen (in Rack Position 2). Or cook it on the pizza stone available for purchase on the Cuisinart website.

Broiling: Broiling function can be used for beef, chicken, pork, fish and more. It also can be used to top-brown casseroles and gratins. Convection Broil is best for meats and fish, while traditional broil should be reserved for top browning.

Toasting: Always have the Oven Rack in Position 2, as indicated in the diagram at right, for even toasting. Always position your item/items in the middle of the rack.

Caution: Aluminum foil is not recommended for covering the AirFryer Toaster Oven accessories. If covered, the foil prevents the fat from dripping into the Drip Tray.
Grease will accumulate on the foil surface and may catch fire. If you choose to use

foil to cover the Baking Pan/Drip Tray, be sure foil is cut to neatly fit into the pan and does not touch the wall or heating elements.

WARNING: Placing the Oven Rack in Position 1 or 2 with the rack upward while toasting may result in a fire. Refer to rack position diagram for proper use. Turning off the AirFryer Toaster Oven: Turn BOTH the ON/Oven Timer and the ON/Toast Timer dials to the OFF position. The power light will turn off.

OPERATION

Unwind the power cord. Check that the Crumb Tray is in place and that there is nothing in the oven. Plug power cord into the wall outlet.

Broil or Convection Broil

Place the AirFryer Basket on top of the Baking Pan to use to Broil in Rack Position 2.

Set the Function Dial to either Broil or Convection Broil. Set Temperature Dial to Toast/Broil. Then turn the ON/Oven Timer dial to the desired cooking time to turn on the oven and begin broiling. The power light will illuminate. The timer will ring once when the cycle is complete and the oven will power off when the time expires. To stop broiling, turn the ON/Oven Timer dial to the OFF position.

Broiling Tips:

For best results, use the provided AirFryer Basket fitted inside the Baking Pan to broil.

Never use glass oven dishes to broil.

Be sure to keep an eye on food – items can get dark quickly while broiling.

Bake or Convection Bake

Fit the Baking Pan or Oven Rack into either rack position.

Set the Function Dial to Bake or Convection Bake. Set the Temperature Dial to desired temperature. Then turn the ON/Oven Timer dial to the recommended cooking time to turn on the oven. It's recommended to preheat oven for 5 minutes prior to baking delicate items such as cakes and muffins. (Incorporate this time into the total baking time.)

The power light will illuminate. The timer will ring once when time has expired and cycle is complete; the oven will power off.

To stop baking mid-cycle, turn the ON/Oven Timer dial to the OFF position.

Baking Tips:

Select Bake for more delicate items like custards, cakes and eggs.

Most baked goods, as well as larger items like chicken, are baked in rack Position 1.

Use Baking Pan in Position 1 for fresh pizza. Place frozen pizza directly on the Rack in Position 2 to cook.

Convection Baking Tips:

Select Convection Bake for hearty baked goods that require even browning such as scones and breads, as well as for roasts and poultry. Convection Bake is also perfect for baking evenly browned and crispy homemade pizzas.

Most recipes recommend reducing heat or temperature by 25°F when Convection Baking.

Always check for doneness 10 minutes before end of suggested cooking time.

IMPORTANT

All of our recipes have been tested in our test kitchen and are specially developed to work in the Cuisinart AirFryer Toaster Oven.

Warm

Fit provided Baking Pan or Oven Rack into Rack Position 2.

Set the Temperature Dial to Warm. Set the Function Dial to Warm. Then turn the ON/Oven Timer Dial to the desired warming time to start the oven and begin warming.

The power light will illuminate. The timer will ring once when the cycle is complete and the oven will power off when the time expires.

To stop warming, turn the ON/Oven Timer dial to the OFF position.

Toast

Fit Oven Rack into Position 2. If toasting two items, center them in the middle of the Oven Rack. Four items should be evenly spaced – two in front, two in back. Six items should be evenly spaced – three in front, three in back.

Set the Function Dial to Toast. Set the Temperature Dial to Toast/Broil. Turn the ON/Toast Timer Dial to desired shade setting from light to dark within the marked settings to turn on the oven and begin toasting.

The oven power light will illuminate. When completed, the timer will ring and turn off.

To stop toasting, turn the ON/Toast Timer dial to the OFF position.

IMPORTANT NOTES ON TOASTING

AirFry

Place the AirFryer Basket onto the Baking Pan. AirFry in Rack Position 2.

Set the Function Dial to AirFry. Set Temperature Dial to desired temperature. Then turn the ON/Oven Timer dial to the desired cooking time to turn on the oven and begin AirFrying.

The oven power light will illuminate. The timer will ring once when the cycle is complete, and the oven will power off when the time expires.

To stop AirFrying, turn the ON/Oven Timer dial to the OFF position.

AirFrying Tips:

AirFrying is a healthy alternative to frying. Many foods that can be fried, can be AirFried without using excess amounts of oil. AirFried foods will taste lighter and less greasy than deep-fried foods.

Most oils can be used for AirFrying. Olive oil is preferred for a richer flavor. Vegetable, canola or grapeseed oil is recommended for a mild flavor.

Distribute oil evenly on food to achieve the crispiest and most golden results. Oil can be sprayed or brushed onto foods for AirFrying. Alternatively, olive oil and non stick cooking sprays can be used.

An assortment of coatings can be used on AirFry foods.

Some examples of different crumb mixtures include: breadcrumbs, seasoned breadcrumbs, panko breadcrumbs, cornflakes, potato chip crumbs, graham cracker crumbs, quinoa, various flours, etc.

Most foods do not need to be flipped during cooking, but larger items, like chicken cutlets, should be flipped halfway during cooking to ensure quick, even cooking and browning.

When AirFrying large quantities of food that crowd the pan, toss food halfway through cooking to ensure even cooking and coloring.

Use higher temperatures for foods that cook quickly, like bacon and chips, and lower temperatures for foods that take longer to cook like breaded chicken.

Foods will cook more evenly if they are cut to the same size. Line the Baking Tray with

aluminum foil for easy cleanup.

Please note that when most foods cook, they release water. When cooking large quantities for an extended period of time, condensation may build up, which could leave moisture on your countertop.

CLEANING AND MAINTENANCE

Always allow the oven to cool completely before cleaning. Always unplug the oven from the electrical outlet.

Do not use abrasive cleaners, as they will damage the finish. Simply wipe the exterior with a clean, damp cloth and dry thoroughly. Apply the
cleansing agent to a cloth, not directly onto the toaster oven, before cleaning.

To clean interior walls, use a damp cloth and a mild liquid soap solution or a spray solution on a sponge. Never use harsh abrasives or corrosive
products. These could damage the oven surface. Never use steel wool pads, etc., on interior of oven.

Oven Rack, Baking Pan, AirFryer Basket and Crumb Tray should be
hand-washed in hot, sudsy water or use a nylon scouring pad or nylon brush. They are NOT dishwasher safe.

After cooking greasy foods and after your oven has cooled, always clean top interior of oven. If this is done on a regular basis, your oven will perform like new. Removing the grease will help to keep toasting consistent, cycle after cycle.

To remove crumbs, slide out the Crumb Tray and discard crumbs. Wipe clean and replace. To remove baked-on grease, soak the tray in hot, sudsy water or use nonabrasive cleaners. Never operate the oven without the Crumb Tray in place.

Never wrap the cord around the outside of the oven. Use the cord storage cleats on the back of the oven.

Any other servicing should be performed by an authorized service representative.

BREAKFAST ANd BRUNCH RECIPES

EGGS WITH TURKEY & SPINACH

Total Time: 38 minutes
Serves: 4
Ingredients
- 1 tablespoon unsalted butter
- 1 lb. fresh baby spinach
- 4 eggs
- 7 oz. cooked turkey, chopped
- 4 teaspoons milk
- Salt and ground black pepper, as required

Directions
1. In a skillet, melt the butter over medium heat and cook the spinach for about 2-3 minutes or until just wilted.
2. Remove from the heat and transfer the spinach into a bowl.
3. Set aside to cool slightly.
4. Divide the spinach into 4 greased ramekins, followed by the turkey.
5. Crack 1 egg into each ramekin and drizzle with milk.
6. Sprinkle with salt and black pepper.
7. Press "Power Button" of Air Fry Oven and turn the dial to select the "Air Fry" mode.
8. Press the Time button and again turn the dial to set the cooking time to 20 minutes.
9. Now push the Temp button and rotate the dial to set the temperature at 355 degrees F.
10. Press "Start/Pause" button to start.
11. When the unit beeps to show that it is preheated, open the lid.
12. Arrange ramekins over the "Wire Rack" and insert in the oven.
13. Serve hot.

EGGS WITH HAM & VEGGIES

Total Time: 30minutes
Serves: 2

Ingredients
- 1 teaspoon olive oil
- 6 small button mushroom, quartered
- 6 cherry tomatoes, halved
- 4 slices shaved ham
- 2 tablespoons spinach, chopped
- 1 cup cheddar cheese, shredded
- 2 eggs
- 1 tablespoon fresh rosemary, chopped
- Salt and ground black pepper, as required

Directions
1. In a skillet, heat the oil over medium heat and cook the mushrooms for about 6-7 minutes.
2. Remove from the heat and set aside to cool slightly.
3. In a bowl, mix together the mushrooms, tomatoes, ham and greens.
4. Place half of the vegetable mixture in a greased baking pan and top with half of the cheese.
5. Repeat the layers once.
6. Make 2 wells in the mixture.
7. Carefully, crack 1 eggs in each well and sprinkle with rosemary, salt and black pepper.
8. Press "Power Button" of Air Fry Oven and turn the dial to select the "Air Fry" mode.
9. Press the Time button and again turn the dial to set the cooking time to 8 minutes.
10. Now push the Temp button and rotate the dial to set the temperature at 390 degrees F.
11. Press "Start/Pause" button to start.
12. When the unit beeps to show that it is preheated, open the lid.
13. Arrange ramekins over the "Wire Rack" and insert in the oven.
14. Serve hot.

EGGS IN BREAd & TOMATO CUPS

Total Time: 27 minutes
Serves: 2
Ingredients

- ½ teaspoon butter
- 2 bread slices
- 1 pancetta slice, chopped
- 4 tomato slices
- 1 tablespoon Mozzarella cheese, shredded
- 2 eggs
- 1/8 teaspoon maple syrup
- 1/8 teaspoon balsamic vinegar
- ¼ teaspoon fresh parsley, chopped
- Salt and freshly ground pepper, to taste

Directions

1. Line each prepared ramekin with 1 bread slice.
2. Divide bacon and tomato slices over bread slice evenly in each ramekin.
3. Top with the cheese evenly.
4. Crack 1 egg in each ramekin over cheese.
5. Drizzle with maple syrup and balsamic vinegar and then sprinkle with parsley, salt and black pepper.
6. Press "Power Button" of Air Fry Oven and turn the dial to select the "Air Fry" mode.
7. Press the Time button and again turn the dial to set the cooking time to 12 minutes.
8. Now push the Temp button and rotate the dial to set the temperature at 320 degrees F.
9. Press "Start/Pause" button to start.
10. When the unit beeps to show that it is preheated, open the lid.
11. Arrange the ramekins over the "Wire Rack" and insert in the oven.
12. Serve warm.

EGGS IN BREAd & SAUSAGE CUPS

Total Time: 32 minutes
Serves: 2
Ingredients
- ¼ cup cream
- 3 eggs
- 2 cooked sausages, sliced
- 1 bread slice, cut into sticks

- ¼ cup mozzarella cheese, grated

Directions
1. In a bowl, add the cream and eggs and beat well.
2. Transfer the egg mixture into ramekins.
3. Place the sausage slices and bread sticks around the edges and gently push them in the egg mixture.
4. Sprinkle with the cheese evenly.
5. Press "Power Button" of Air Fry Oven and turn the dial to select the "Air Fry" mode.
6. Press the Time button and again turn the dial to set the cooking time to 22 minutes.
7. Now push the Temp button and rotate the dial to set the temperature at 355 degrees F.
8. Press "Start/Pause" button to start.
9. When the unit beeps to show that it is preheated, open the lid.
10. Arrange the ramekins over the "Wire Rack" and insert in the oven.
11. Serve warm.

EGGS IN BREAd & BACON CUPS

Total Time: 25 minutes
Serves: 4
Ingredients
- 4 bacon slices
- 4 bread slices
- 1 scallion, chopped
- 2 tablespoons bell pepper, seeded and chopped
- 1½ tablespoons mayonnaise
- 4 eggs

Directions
1. Grease 6 cups muffin tin with cooking spray.
2. Line the sides of each prepared muffin cup with 1 bacon slice.
3. Cut bread slices with round cookie cutter.
4. Arrange the bread slice in the bottom of each muffin cup.
5. Top with, scallion, bell pepper and mayonnaise evenly.
6. Carefully, crack one egg in each muffin cup.

7. Press "Power Button" of Air Fry Oven and turn the dial to select the "Air Fry" mode.
8. Press the Time button and again turn the dial to set the cooking time to 15 minutes.
9. Now push the Temp button and rotate the dial to set the temperature at 375 degrees F.
10. Press "Start/Pause" button to start.
11. When the unit beeps to show that it is preheated, open the lid.
12. Arrange the ramekins over the "Wire Rack" and insert in the oven.
13. Serve warm.

SPINACH & MOZZARELLA MUFFINS

Total Time: 20 minutes
Serves: 2
Ingredients
- 2 large eggs
- 2 tablespoons half-and-half
- 2 tablespoons frozen spinach, thawed
- 4 teaspoons mozzarella cheese, grated
- Salt and ground black pepper, as required

Directions
1. Grease 2 ramekins.
2. In each prepared ramekin, crack 1 egg.
3. Divide the half-and-half, spinach, cheese, salt and black pepper and each ramekin and gently stir to combine, without breaking the yolks.
4. Press "Power Button" of Air Fry Oven and turn the dial to select the "Air Fry" mode.
5. Press the Time button and again turn the dial to set the cooking time to 10 minutes.
6. Now push the Temp button and rotate the dial to set the temperature at 330 degrees F.
7. Press "Start/Pause" button to start.
8. When the unit beeps to show that it is preheated, open the lid.
9. Arrange the ramekins over the "Wire Rack" and insert in the oven.
10. Serve warm.

BACON & SPINACH MUFFINS

Total Time: 27 minutes
Serves: 6
Ingredients
- 6 eggs
- ½ cup milk
- Salt and ground black pepper, as required
- 1 cup fresh spinach, chopped
- 4 cooked bacon slices, crumbled

Directions
1. In a bowl, add the eggs, milk, salt and black pepper and beat until well combined.
2. Add the spinach and stir to combine.
3. Divide the spinach mixture into 6 greased cups of an egg bite mold evenly.
4. Press "Power Button" of Air Fry Oven and turn the dial to select the "Air Fry" mode.
5. Press the Time button and again turn the dial to set the cooking time to 17 minutes.
6. Now push the Temp button and rotate the dial to set the temperature at 325 degrees F.
7. Press "Start/Pause" button to start.
8. When the unit beeps to show that it is preheated, open the lid.
9. Arrange the mold over the "Wire Rack" and insert in the oven.
10. Place the mold onto a wire rack to cool for about 5 minutes.
11. Top with bacon pieces and serve warm.

HAM MUFFINS

Total Time: 28 minutes
Serves: 6
Ingredients
- 6 ham slices
- 6 eggs
- 6 tablespoons cream

- 3 tablespoon mozzarella cheese, shredded
- ¼ teaspoon dried basil, crushed

Directions

1. Lightly, grease 6 cups of a silicone muffin tin.
2. Line each prepared muffin cup with 1 ham slice.
3. Crack 1 egg into each muffin cup and top with cream.
4. Sprinkle with cheese and basil.
5. Press "Power Button" of Air Fry Oven and turn the dial to select the "Air Fry" mode.
6. Press the Time button and again turn the dial to set the cooking time to 18 minutes.
7. Now push the Temp button and rotate the dial to set the temperature at 350 degrees F.
8. Press "Start/Pause" button to start.
9. When the unit beeps to show that it is preheated, open the lid.
10. Arrange the muffin tin over the "Wire Rack" and insert in the oven.
11. Place the muffin tin onto a wire rack to cool for about 5 minutes.
12. Carefully, invert the muffins onto the platter and serve warm.

SAVORY CARROT MUFFINS

Total Time: 22 minutes
Serves: 6
Ingredients

For Muffins:

- ¼ cup whole-wheat flour
- ¼ cup all-purpose flour
- ½ teaspoon baking powder
- 1/8 teaspoon baking soda
- ½ teaspoon dried parsley, crushed
- ½ teaspoon salt
- ½ cup plain yogurt
- 1 teaspoon vinegar
- 1 tablespoon vegetable oil
- 3 tablespoons cottage cheese, grated

- 1 carrot, peeled and grated
- 2-4 tablespoons water (if needed)

For Topping:

- 7 oz. Parmesan cheese, grated
- ¼ cup walnuts, chopped

Directions

1. For muffin: in a large bowl, mix together the flours, baking powder, baking soda, parsley, and salt.
2. In another large bowl, mix well the yogurt, and vinegar.
3. Add the remaining ingredients except water and beat them well. (add some water if needed)
4. Make a well in the center of the yogurt mixture.
5. Slowly, add the flour mixture in the well and mix until well combined.
6. Place the mixture into lightly greased muffin molds evenly and top with the Parmesan cheese and walnuts.
7. Press "Power Button" of Air Fry Oven and turn the dial to select the "Air Fry" mode.
8. Press the Time button and again turn the dial to set the cooking time to 7 minutes.
9. Now push the Temp button and rotate the dial to set the temperature at 355 degrees F.
10. Press "Start/Pause" button to start.
11. When the unit beeps to show that it is preheated, open the lid.
12. Arrange the ramekins over "Wire Rack" and insert in the oven.
13. Place the muffin molds onto a wire rack to cool for about 5 minutes.
14. Carefully, invert the muffins onto the platter and serve warm.

POTATO & BELL PEPPER HASH

Total Time: 40 minutes
Serves: 4
Ingredients
- 2 cups water
- 5 russet potatoes, peeled and cubed
- ½ tablespoon extra-virgin olive oil
- ½ of onion, chopped
- ½ of jalapeño, chopped
- 1 green bell pepper, seeded and chopped
- ¼ teaspoon dried oregano, crushed
- ¼ teaspoon garlic powder
- ¼ teaspoon ground cumin
- ¼ teaspoon red chili powder
- Salt and freshly ground black pepper, as needed

Directions
1. In a large bowl, add the water and potatoes and set aside for about 30 minutes.
2. Drain well and pat dry with the paper towels.
3. In a bowl, add the potatoes and oil and toss to coat well.
4. Press "Power Button" of Air Fry Oven and turn the dial to select the "Air Fry" mode.
5. Press the Time button and again turn the dial to set the cooking time to 5 minutes.
6. Now push the Temp button and rotate the dial to set the temperature at 330 degrees F.
7. Press "Start/Pause" button to start.
8. When the unit beeps to show that it is preheated, open the lid.
9. Arrange the potato cubes in "Air Fry Basket" and insert in the oven.
10. Transfer the potatoes onto a plate.
11. In a bowl, add the potatoes and remaining ingredients and toss to coat well.
12. Press "Power Button" of Air Fry Oven and turn the dial to select the "Air Fry" mode.
13. Press the Time button and again turn the dial to set the cooking time to 20 minutes.

14. Now push the Temp button and rotate the dial to set the temperature at 390 degrees F.
15. Press "Start/Pause" button to start.
16. When the unit beeps to show that it is preheated, open the lid.
17. Arrange the veggie mixture in "Air Fry Basket" and insert in the oven.
18. Serve hot.

APPLE FRITTER LOAF

Total Time: 75 minutes

Serves: 10

Ingredients
- Butter flavored cooking spray
- 1/3 cup brown sugar, packed
- 1 tsp. cinnamon, divided
- 1 ½ cups apples, chopped
- 2/3 cup + 1 tsp. sugar, divided
- ½ cup + ½ tbsp. butter, soft, divided
- 2 eggs
- 2 ¼ tsp. vanilla, divided
- 1 ½ cups flour
- 2 tsp baking powder
- ¼ tsp salt
- ½ cup + 2 tbsp. milk
- 1/2 cup powdered sugar

Directions
1. Place rack in position 1 of the oven. Spray an 8-inch loaf pan with cooking spray.
2. In a small bowl, combine brown sugar and ½ teaspoon cinnamon.
3. Place apples in a medium bowl and sprinkle with remaining cinnamon and 1 teaspoon sugar, toss to coat.
4. In a large bowl, beat remaining sugar and butter until smooth.
5. Beat in eggs and 2 teaspoons vanilla until combined. Stir in flour, baking powder, and salt until combined.

6. Add ½ cup milk and beat until smooth. Pour half the batter in the prepared pan. Add half the apples then remaining batter. Add the remaining apples over the top, pressing lightly. Sprinkle brown sugar mixture over the apples.
7. Set oven to convection bake at 325°F for 5 minutes. Once timer goes, off place bread on the rack and set timer to 1 hour. Bread is done when it passes the toothpick test.
8. Let cool in pan 10 minutes, then invert onto wire rack to cool.
9. In a small bowl, whisk together powdered sugar and butter until smooth. Whisk in remaining milk and vanilla and drizzle over cooled bread.

ENCHILAdAS 4 BREAKFAST

Total Time: 50minutes

Serves: 8

Ingredients
- Nonstick cooking spray
- 1 lb. pork breakfast sausage
- 2 cups hash browns, thawed
- 1/3 cup red bell pepper, chopped
- 1/3 cup poblano pepper, chopped
- 6 green onion, sliced thin
- 2 tsp garlic salt divided
- 10 eggs
- 1 tsp black pepper
- 3 cups pepper jack cheese, grated
- 8 8-inch
- 1 cup salsa Verde
- ½ cup half & half
- ½ tsp cumin
- ½ tsp oregano

Directions
1. Place the rack in position 1. Lightly spray an 8x11-inch baking dish with cooking spray.
2. In a medium saucepan, over medium heat, cook sausage until no longer pink. Use a slotted spoon to transfer to a paper towel lined plate.

3. Add potatoes, red pepper, poblano, 1 teaspoon garlic salt, and onion (saving 3 tablespoons for garnish) to the pan. Cook until vegetables are fork-tender, about 5-7 minutes. Stir in sausage and stir to combine. Remove from heat.
4. In a medium bowl, whisk eggs, remaining garlic salt, and pepper.
5. Heat a medium skillet over medium heat. Once hot, add eggs and scramble until done. Remove from heat.
6. Place tortillas, one at a time, on work surface. Use 2 cups of cheese for filling. Sprinkle some cheese down the middle. Top with sausage mixture and a little more cheese. Roll up and place seam side down in prepared pan. Repeat with remaining ingredients.
7. In a small bowl, whisk together salsa Verde, half & half, cumin, and oregano. Pour over enchiladas and top with remaining cheese.
8. Set to bake on 375°F for 35 minutes. After 5 minutes, place baking pan on rack and bake 30 minutes or until golden brown and bubbly. Serve garnished with reserved onions.

CINNAMON STREUSEL BREAd

Total Time: 90 minutes

Serves: 8

Ingredients
- 1 cup warm water
- 1 envelope yeast, quick rising
- 1/3 cup + 6 tsp milk, divided
- 1 egg
- 3 tbsp. sugar
- 2 tbsp. butter, cold & cut in cubes
- 1 cup powdered sugar
- 3 ½ cups flour, divided
- 1 tbsp. + 2 tsp olive oil
- 1 tsp salt
- 2 tbsp. cinnamon
- ½ cup brown sugar

Directions
1. In a large bowl, add water and sprinkle yeast over top, stir to dissolve.
2. Stir in 1/3 cup milk, egg, and sugar until combined.
3. Add 2 cups flour and stir in until batter gets thick. With a wooden spoon, or mixer with dough hook attached, beat 100 strokes.
4. Fold in oil and salt. Then stir in 1 ¼ cups flour until dough begins to come together.
5. Mix in cinnamon and transfer dough to a lightly floured work surface. Knead for 5

minutes then form into a ball.
6. Use remaining oil to grease a clean bowl and add dough. Cover and let rise 30 minutes.
7. Spray a 9-inch loaf pan with cooking spray.
8. After 30 minutes, punch dough down and divide into 8 equal pieces.
9. Place brown sugar in a shallow bowl and roll dough pieces in it, forming it into balls. Place in prepared pan and sprinkle remaining brown sugar over top.
10. In a small bowl, combine butter and ¼ cup flour until mixture resembles coarse crumbs. Sprinkle over top of bread.
11. Place rack in position 1 of the oven. Set to convection bake on 325°F and set timer for 35 minutes. After 5 minutes, add pan to the rack and bake 30 minutes or until golden brown.
12. Let cool in pan 10 minutes, then invert onto wire rack.
13. In a small bowl, whisk together powdered sugar and milk until smooth. Drizzle over warm bread and serve.

BRIOCHE BREAKFAST PUddING

Total Time: 55 minutes

Serves: 8

Ingredients
- 1 loaf brioche bread, cut in cubes
- ½ tbsp. coconut oil, soft
- 4 cups milk
- 1 can coconut milk
- 6 eggs
- ½ cup sugar
- 2 tsp vanilla
- ¼ tsp salt
- 1 cup coconut, shredded
- ½ cup chocolate chips

Directions
1. Place rack in position 1 of the oven. Grease an 8x11-inch baking pan with coconut oil.
2. Add the bread cubes to the pan, pressing lightly to settle.
3. In a large bowl, whisk together milk, coconut milk, eggs, sugar, vanilla, and salt until combined.
4. Stir in coconut and chocolate chips. Pour evenly over bread. Cover with plastic wrap and refrigerate 2 hours or overnight.

5. Set oven to bake on 350°F for 50 minutes. After 5 minutes, add the pudding to the oven and bake 40-45 minutes, or until top is beginning to brown and it passes the toothpick test.
6. Remove to wire rack and let cool 5-10 minutes before serving.

STRAWBERRY BASIL MUFFINS

Total Time: 35 minutes

Serves: 12

Ingredients
- 3 tbsp. almonds
- ¾ cup + 2 tbsp. flour, divided
- ½ cup + 2 tbsp. brown sugar, divided
- ½ tsp salt, divided
- ¼ cup + 2 tbsp. coconut oil, melted
- 1 cup white whole-wheat flour
- 2 tsp baking powder
- 1 tsp baking soda
- 1 ¼ cup buttermilk, low fat
- 1 egg
- 1 tsp vanilla
- 1 ½ cups strawberries, chopped
- ¼ cup fresh basil, chopped

Directions
1. Place rack in position 1 of the oven. Line 2 6-cup muffin tins with paper liners.
2. Place almonds, 2 tablespoons flour, 2 tablespoons brown sugar, and ¼ teaspoon salt in the food processor or blender. Pulse until finely ground. Transfer to a small bowl and stir in 2 tablespoons oil until combined.
3. In a large bowl, combine remaining flour, whole wheat flour, baking powder, baking soda, and remaining salt together.
4. In a separate large bowl, whisk together, remaining brown sugar, oil, buttermilk, juice, egg and vanilla until thoroughly combined.
5. Make a well in the dry ingredients and add wet ingredients, stir just until combined.

6. Fold in berries and basil. Divide evenly between prepared pans. Sprinkle almond topping over muffins.
7. Set oven to bake on 400°F for 25 minutes. After 5 minutes, add muffin tins, one at a time, to oven and bake 18-20 minutes or until muffins pass the toothpick test. Let cool in pan 10 minutes, then transfer to wire rack to cool completely.

POULTRY RECIPES

ROASTEd GOOSE

Total Time: 50 minutes
Serves: 12
Ingredients
- 8 lbs. goose
- Juice of a lemon
- Salt and pepper
- 1/2 yellow onion, peeled and chopped
- 1 head garlic, peeled and chopped
- 1/2 cup wine
- 1 teaspoon dried thyme

Directions
1. Place the goose in a baking tray and whisk the rest of the ingredients in a bowl.
2. Pour this thick sauce over the goose and brush it liberally.
3. Press "Power Button" of Air Fry Oven and turn the dial to select the "Air Roast" mode.
4. Press the Time button and again turn the dial to set the cooking time to 40 minutes.
5. Now push the Temp button and rotate the dial to set the temperature at 355 degrees F.
6. Once preheated, place the casserole dish inside and close its lid.
7. Serve warm.

CHRISTMAS ROAST GOOSE

Total Time: 70 minutes
Serves: 12
Ingredients
- 2 goose
- 2 lemons, sliced
- 1 ½ lime, sliced
- ½ teaspoon Chinese five-spice powder

- ½ handful parsley, chopped
- ½ handful sprigs, chopped
- ½ handful thyme, chopped
- ½ handful sage, chopped
- 1 ½ tablespoon clear honey
- ½ tablespoon thyme leaves

Directions
1. Place the goose in a baking dish and brush it with honey.
2. Set the lemon and lime slices on top of the goose.
3. Add all the herbs and spice powder over the lemon slices.
4. Press "Power Button" of Air Fry Oven and turn the dial to select the "Air Roast" mode.
5. Press the Time button and again turn the dial to set the cooking time to 60 minutes.
6. Now push the Temp button and rotate the dial to set the temperature at 375 degrees F.
7. Once preheated, place the baking dish inside and close its lid.
8. Serve warm.

CHICKEN KEBABS

Total Time: 30 minutes
Serves: 2
Ingredients
- 16 oz skinless chicken breasts, cubed
- 2 tablespoons soy sauce
- ½ zucchini sliced
- 1 tablespoon chicken seasoning
- 1 teaspoon bbq seasoning
- salt and pepper to taste
- ½ green pepper sliced
- ½ red pepper sliced
- ½ yellow pepper sliced
- ¼ red onion sliced
- 4 cherry tomatoes
- cooking spray

Directions
1. Toss chicken and veggies with all the spices and seasoning in a bowl.
2. Alternatively, thread them on skewers and place these skewers in the Air fryer basket.

3. Press "Power Button" of Air Fry Oven and turn the dial to select the "Air Fry" mode.
4. Press the Time button and again turn the dial to set the cooking time to 20 minutes.
5. Now push the Temp button and rotate the dial to set the temperature at 350 degrees F.
6. Once preheated, place the baking dish inside and close its lid.
7. Flip the skewers when cooked halfway through then resume cooking.
8. Serve warm.

ASIAN CHICKEN KEBABS

Total Time: 22 minutes
Serves: 6
Ingredients
- 2 lbs. chicken breasts, cubed
- 1/2 cup soy sauce
- 6 cloves garlic, crushed
- 1 teaspoon fresh ginger, grated
- 1/2 cup golden sweetener
- 1 red pepper, chopped
- 1/2 red onion, chopped
- 8 mushrooms, halved
- 2 cups zucchini, chopped

Directions
1. Toss chicken and veggies with all the spices and seasoning in a bowl.
2. Alternatively, thread them on skewers and place these skewers in the Air fryer basket.
3. Press "Power Button" of Air Fry Oven and turn the dial to select the "Air Fry" mode.
4. Press the Time button and again turn the dial to set the cooking time to 12 minutes.
5. Now push the Temp button and rotate the dial to set the temperature at 380 degrees F.
6. Once preheated, place the baking dish inside and close its lid.
7. Flip the skewers when cooked halfway through then resume cooking.
8. Serve warm.

KEBAB TAVUK SHEESH

Total Time: 20 minutes
Serves: 2
Ingredients
- 1/4 cup plain yogurt
- 1 tablespoon garlic, minced
- 1 tablespoon tomato paste
- 1 tablespoon olive oil
- 1 tablespoon lemon juice
- 1 teaspoon salt
- 1 teaspoon ground cumin
- 1 teaspoon smoked paprika
- 1/2 teaspoon ground cinnamon
- 1/2 teaspoon ground black pepper
- 1/2 teaspoon cayenne
- 1 lb. boneless skinless chicken thighs, quartered

Directions
1. Mix chicken with yogurt and all the seasonings in a bowl.
2. Marinate the yogurt chicken for 30 minutes in the refrigerator.
3. Thread chicken pieces on the skewers and place these skewers in the Air fryer basket.
4. Press "Power Button" of Air Fry Oven and turn the dial to select the "Air Fry" mode.
5. Press the Time button and again turn the dial to set the cooking time to 10 minutes.
6. Now push the Temp button and rotate the dial to set the temperature at 370 degrees F.
7. Once preheated, place the baking dish inside and close its lid.
8. Flip the skewers when cooked halfway through then resume cooking.
9. Serve warm.

CHICKEN MUSHROOM KEBAB

Total Time: 25 minutes
Serves: 4
Ingredients
- 1/3 cup honey

- 1/3 cup soy sauce
- Salt, to taste
- 6 mushrooms chop in half
- 3 bell peppers, cubed
- 2 chicken breasts diced

Directions
1. Toss chicken, mushrooms and veggies with all the honey, and seasoning in a bowl.
2. Alternatively, thread them on skewers and place these skewers in the Air fryer basket.
3. Press "Power Button" of Air Fry Oven and turn the dial to select the "Air Fry" mode.
4. Press the Time button and again turn the dial to set the cooking time to 15 minutes.
5. Now push the Temp button and rotate the dial to set the temperature at 350 degrees F.
6. Once preheated, place the baking dish inside and close its lid.
7. Flip the skewers when cooked halfway through then resume cooking.
8. Serve warm.

CHICKEN FAJITA SKEWERS

Total Time: 18 minutes
Serves: 2
Ingredients
- 1 lb. chicken breasts, diced
- 1 tablespoon lemon juice
- 1 teaspoon chili powder
- 1 teaspoon cumin
- 1 orange bell pepper, cut into squares
- 1 red bell pepper, cut into squares
- 2 tablespoon olive oil
- 1 teaspoon garlic powder
- 1 large red onion, cut into squares
- 1 teaspoon salt
- 1 teaspoon ground black pepper
- 1 teaspoon oregano
- 1 teaspoon parsley flakes
- 1 teaspoon paprika

Directions
1. Toss chicken and veggies with all the spices and seasoning in a bowl.
2. Alternatively, thread them on skewers and place these skewers in the Air fryer basket.
3. Press "Power Button" of Air Fry Oven and turn the dial to select the "Air Fry" mode.
4. Press the Time button and again turn the dial to set the cooking time to 8 minutes.
5. Now push the Temp button and rotate the dial to set the temperature at 360 degrees F.
6. Once preheated, place the baking dish inside and close its lid.
7. Flip the skewers when cooked halfway through then resume cooking.
8. Serve warm.

ZUCCHINI CHICKEN KEBABS

Total Time: 20 minutes
Serves: 4
Ingredients
- 1 large zucchini, cut into squares
- 2 chicken breasts boneless, skinless, cubed
- 1 onion yellow, cut into squares
- 1.5 cup grape tomatoes
- 1 clove garlic minced
- 1 lemon juiced
- 1/4 c olive oil
- 1 tablespoon olive oil
- 2 tablespoon red wine vinegar
- 1 teaspoon oregano

Directions
1. Toss chicken and veggies with all the spices and seasoning in a bowl.
2. Alternatively, thread them on skewers and place these skewers in the Air fryer basket.
3. Press "Power Button" of Air Fry Oven and turn the dial to select the "Air Fry" mode.
4. Press the Time button and again turn the dial to set the cooking time to 16 minutes.
5. Now push the Temp button and rotate the dial to set the temperature at 380 degrees F.
6. Once preheated, place the baking dish inside and close its lid.
7. Flip the skewers when cooked halfway through then resume cooking.

8. Serve warm.

CHICKEN SOY SKEWERS

Total Time: 17 minutes
Serves: 4
Ingredients
- 1-lb. boneless chicken tenders, diced
- 1/2 cup soy sauce
- 1/2 cup pineapple juice
- 1/4 cup sesame seed oil
- 2 teaspoons toasted sesame seeds
- black pepper
- 4 garlic cloves, chopped
- 4 scallions, chopped
- 1 tablespoon grated ginger

Directions
1. Toss chicken with all the sauces and seasonings in a baking pan.
2. Press "Power Button" of Air Fry Oven and turn the dial to select the "Air Fry" mode.
3. Press the Time button and again turn the dial to set the cooking time to 7 minutes.
4. Now push the Temp button and rotate the dial to set the temperature at 390 degrees F.
5. Once preheated, place the baking dish inside and close its lid.
6. Serve warm.

CHICKEN ALFREdO BAKE

Total Time: 35 minutes
Serves: 6
Ingredients
- 1 tablespoon olive oil
- 3 chicken breasts, cubed
- salt, to taste
- Black pepper, to taste

- 4 cloves garlic, minced
- 2 ½ cups chicken broth
- 2 ½ cups heavy cream
- 1 handful fresh parsley, chopped
- 1 cup penne pasta, uncooked
- 2 cups parmesan cheese
- 2 cups mozzarella cheese

Directions
1. Whisk cream, broth, chicken, pasta, and all the ingredients in a casserole dish.
2. Press "Power Button" of Air Fry Oven and turn the dial to select the "Bake" mode.
3. Press the Time button and again turn the dial to set the cooking time to 25 minutes.
4. Now push the Temp button and rotate the dial to set the temperature at 380 degrees F.
5. Once preheated, place the baking dish inside and close its lid.
6. Serve warm.

BUFFALO CHICKEN TENDERS

Total Time: 85 minutes

Serves: 5

Ingredients
- Nonstick cooking spray
- 2/3 cup panko bread crumbs
- ½ tsp cayenne pepper
- ½ tsp paprika
- ½ tsp garlic powder
- ½ tsp salt
- 3 chicken breasts, boneless, skinless & cut in 10 strips
- ½ cup butter, melted
- ½ cup hot sauce

Directions
1. Line a baking sheet with foil and spray with cooking spray.
2. In a shallow dish combine, bread crumbs and seasonings.
3. Dip chicken in crumb mixture to coat all sides. Lay on prepared pan and refrigerate 1 hour.
4. In a small bowl, whisk together butter and hot sauce.
5. Place baking pan in position 2 of the oven. Lightly spray the fryer basket with cooking

spray.
6. Dip each piece of chicken in the butter mixture and place in basket. Place the basket on the baking pan.
7. Set oven to air fry on 400°F for 25 minutes. Cook until outside is crispy and golden brown and chicken is no longer pink. Turn chicken over halfway through cooking time. Serve immediately.

TURKEY TURNOVERS

Total Time: 20 minutes

Serves: 8

Ingredients
- 2 cups turkey, cooked & chopped
- 1 cup cheddar cheese, grated
- 1 cup broccoli, cooked & chopped
- ½ cup mayonnaise
- ½ tsp salt
- ¼ tsp pepper
- 2 cans refrigerated crescent rolls

Directions
1. Place the baking pan in position 1 of the oven.
2. In a large bowl, combine all ingredients, except rolls, mix well.
3. Separate each can of rolls into 4 squares, press perforations to seal.
4. Spoon turkey mixture on center of each square. Fold over diagonally and seal the edges.
5. Set oven to bake on 375°F for 15 minutes.
6. Brush tops of turnovers lightly with additional mayonnaise. After oven has preheated 5 minutes, place turnovers on baking pan and cook 10-12 minutes or until golden brown. Serve warm.

CHICKEN PARM

Total Time: 45 minutes

Serves: 4

Ingredients
- Nonstick cooking spray
- ½ cup flour
- 2 eggs
- 2/3 cup panko bread crumbs
- 2/3 cup Italian seasoned bread crumbs
- 1/3 + ¼ cup parmesan cheese, divided
- 2 tbsp. fresh parsley, chopped
- ½ tsp salt
- ¼ tsp pepper
- 4 chicken breast halves, skinless & boneless
- 24 oz. marinara sauce
- 1 cup mozzarella cheese, grated

Directions

1. Place the baking pan in position 2 of the oven. Lightly spray the fryer basket with cooking spray.
2. Place flour in a shallow dish.
3. In a separate shallow dish, beat the eggs.
4. In a third shallow dish, combine both bread crumbs, 1/3 cup parmesan cheese, 2 tablespoons parsley, salt, and pepper.
5. Place chicken between two sheets of plastic wrap and pound to ½-inch thick.
6. Dip chicken first in flour, then eggs, and bread crumb mixture to coat. Place in basket and place the basket on the baking pan.
7. Set oven to air fry on 375°F for 10 minutes. Turn chicken over halfway through cooking time.
8. Remove chicken and baking pan from the oven. Place the rack in position 1. Set oven to bake on 425°F for 30 minutes.
9. Pour 1 ½ cups marinara in the bottom of 8x11-inch baking dish. Place chicken over sauce and add another 2 tablespoons marinara to tops of chicken. Top chicken with mozzarella and parmesan cheese.
10. Once oven preheats for 5 minutes, place the dish in the oven and bake 20-25 minutes until bubbly and cheese is golden brown. Serve.

TERIYAKI DUCK LEGS

Total Time: 135 minutes

Serves: 6

Ingredients
- 3 lbs. duck legs
- ½ cup teriyaki sauce
- 2 tbsp. soy sauce
- 2 tbsp. malt vinegar

Directions
1. Place the rack in position 1 of the oven.
2. Place the duck legs, skin side up, in an 8x11-inch baking dish.
3. In a small bowl, whisk together remaining ingredients and pour around duck legs. Liquid needs to reach the skin level of duck, if not add water until it does.
4. Set the oven to convection bake on 300°F for 60 minutes. After 5 minutes, place the ducks in the oven and cook 90 minutes, or until tender.
5. Remove duck from the oven. Pour off cooking liquid into a small saucepan. Skim off fat and reserve. Bring sauce to a boil and cook until it reduces down, about 10 minutes, stirring occasionally.
6. Place the baking pan in position 2 of the oven. Place the duck legs in the fryer basket and brush with reserved fat and sauce. Place the basket in the oven and set to broil on 400°F for 10 minutes. Turn duck over halfway through and brush with fat and sauce again. Serve.

TURKEY BURGERS

Total Time: 20 minutes

Serves: 4

Ingredients
- 1 1/3 lb. ground turkey
- ½ cup gruyere cheese, grated
- 3 green onions, chopped fine
- ¼ cup bread crumbs
- ¼ cup Dijon mustard
- ½ tsp salt
- ½ tsp pepper

Directions
1. In a large bowl, combine all ingredients until combined.
2. Form into 4 patties. Lightly spray tops with cooking spray and put them in the fryer basket, sprayed side down. Spray patties again.
3. Place the baking pan in position 2 of the oven and add basket. Set oven to air fry on 400°F for 10 minutes. Turn burgers over halfway through cooking time. Serve.

VEGETABLES RECIPES

GLAZEd VEGGIES

Total Time: 35 minutes
Serves: 4
Ingredients
- 2 oz. cherry tomatoes
- 2 large zucchini, chopped
- 2 green bell peppers, seeded and chopped
- 6 tablespoons olive oil, divided
- 2 tablespoons honey
- 1 teaspoon Dijon mustard
- 1 teaspoon dried herbs
- 1 teaspoon garlic paste
- Salt, as required

Directions
1. In a parchment paper-lined baking pan, place the vegetables and drizzle with 3 tablespoons of oil.
2. Press "Power Button" of Air Fry Oven and turn the dial to select the "Air Fry" mode.
3. Press the Time button and again turn the dial to set the cooking time to 15 minutes.
4. Now push the Temp button and rotate the dial to set the temperature at 355 degrees F.
5. Press "Start/Pause" button to start.
6. When the unit beeps to show that it is preheated, open the lid.
7. Arrange the pan over the "Wire Rack" and insert in the oven.
8. Meanwhile, in a bowl, add the remaining oil, honey, mustard, herbs, garlic, salt, and black pepper and mix well.
9. After 15 minutes of cooking, add the honey mixture into vegetable mixture and mix well.
10. Now, set the temperature to 392 degrees F for 5 minutes.
11. Serve immediately.

PARMESAN MIXEd VEGGIES

Total Time: 33 minutes
Serves: 5
Ingredients

- 1 tablespoon olive oil
- 1 tablespoon garlic, minced
- 1 cup cauliflower florets
- 1 cup broccoli florets
- 1 cup zucchini, sliced
- ½ cup yellow squash, sliced
- ½ cup fresh mushrooms, sliced
- 1 small onion, sliced
- ¼ cup balsamic vinegar
- 1 teaspoon red pepper flakes
- Salt and ground black pepper, as required
- ¼ cup Parmesan cheese, grated

Directions
1. In a large bowl, add all the ingredients except cheese and toss to coat well.
2. Press "Power Button" of Air Fry Oven and turn the dial to select the "Air Fry" mode.
3. Press the Time button and again turn the dial to set the cooking time to 18 minutes.
4. Now push the Temp button and rotate the dial to set the temperature at 400 degrees F.
5. Press "Start/Pause" button to start.
6. When the unit beeps to show that it is preheated, open the lid.
7. Arrange the vegetables in greased "Air Fry Basket" and insert in the oven.
8. After 8 minutes of cooking, flip the vegetables.
9. After 16 minutes of cooking, sprinkle the vegetables with cheese evenly.
10. Serve hot.

VEGGIE KABOBS

Total Time: 30 minutes   **Serves:** 6

Ingredients
- ¼ cup carrots, peeled and chopped
- ¼ cup French beans
- ½ cup green peas
- 1 teaspoon ginger
- 3 garlic cloves, peeled
- 2 medium boiled potatoes, mashed
- 3 green chilies
- ¼ cup fresh mint leaves
- ½ cup cottage cheese

- ½ teaspoon five spice powder
- Salt, to taste
- 2 tablespoons corn flour
- Olive oil cooking spray

Directions
1. In a food processor, add the carrot, beans, peas, ginger, garlic, mint, cheese and pulse until smooth.
2. Transfer the mixture into a bowl.
3. Add the potato, five spice powder, salt and corn flour and mix until well combined.
4. Divide the mixture into equal sized small balls.
5. Press each ball around a skewer in a sausage shape.
6. Spray the skewers with cooking spray.
7. Press "Power Button" of Air Fry Oven and turn the dial to select the "Air Fry" mode.
8. Press the Time button and again turn the dial to set the cooking time to 10 minutes.
9. Now push the Temp button and rotate the dial to set the temperature at 390 degrees F.
10. Press "Start/Pause" button to start.
11. When the unit beeps to show that it is preheated, open the lid.
12. Arrange the skewers in greased "Air Fry Basket" and insert in the oven.
13. Serve warm.

BEANS & VEGGIE BURGERS

Total Time: 42 minutes
Serves: 4
Ingredients
- 1 cup cooked black beans
- 2 cups boiled potatoes, peeled and mashed
- 1 cup fresh spinach, chopped
- 1 cup fresh mushrooms, chopped
- 2 teaspoons Chile lime seasoning
- Olive oil cooking spray

Directions
1. In a large bowl, add the beans, potatoes, spinach, mushrooms, and seasoning and with your hands, mix until well combined.
2. Make 4 equal-sized patties from the mixture.

3. Spray the patties with cooking spray evenly.
4. Press "Power Button" of Air Fry Oven and turn the dial to select the "Air Fry" mode.
5. Press the Time button and again turn the dial to set the cooking time to 22 minutes.
6. Now push the Temp button and rotate the dial to set the temperature at 370 degrees F.
7. Press "Start/Pause" button to start.
8. When the unit beeps to show that it is preheated, open the lid.
9. Arrange the skewers in greased "Air Fry Basket" and insert in the oven.
10. Flip the patties once after 12 minutes.

MARINATEd TOFU

Total Time: 40 minutes
Serves: 4
Ingredients
- 2 tablespoon low-sodium soy sauce
- 2 tablespoon fish sauce
- 1 teaspoon olive oil
- 12 oz. extra-firm tofu, drained and cubed into 1-inch size
- 1 teaspoon butter, melted

Directions
1. In a large bowl, add the soy sauce, fish sauce and oil and mix until well combined.
2. Add the tofu cubes and toss to coat well.
3. Set aside to marinate for about 30 minutes, tossing occasionally.
4. Press "Power Button" of Air Fry Oven and turn the dial to select the "Air Fry" mode.
5. Press the Time button and again turn the dial to set the cooking time to 25 minutes.
6. Now push the Temp button and rotate the dial to set the temperature at 355 degrees F.
7. Press "Start/Pause" button to start.
8. When the unit beeps to show that it is preheated, open the lid.
9. Arrange the tofu cubes in greased "Air Fry Basket" and insert in the oven.

10. Flip the tofu after every 10 minutes during the cooking.
11. Serve hot.

CRUSTEd TOFU

Total Time: 43 minutes
Serves: 3
Ingredients
- 1 (14-oz.) block firm tofu, pressed and cubed into ½-inch size
- 2 tablespoons cornstarch
- ¼ cup rice flour
- Salt and ground black pepper, as required
- 2 tablespoons olive oil

Directions
1. In a bowl, mix together the cornstarch, rice flour, salt, and black pepper.
2. Coat the tofu with flour mixture evenly.
3. Then, drizzle the tofu with oil.
4. Press "Power Button" of Air Fry Oven and turn the dial to select the "Air Fry" mode.
5. Press the Time button and again turn the dial to set the cooking time to 28 minutes.
6. Now push the Temp button and rotate the dial to set the temperature at 360 degrees F.
7. Press "Start/Pause" button to start.
8. When the unit beeps to show that it is preheated, open the lid.
9. Arrange the tofu cubes in greased "Air Fry Basket" and insert in the oven.
10. Flip the tofu cubes once halfway through.
11. Serve hot.

TOFU WITH ORANGE SAUCE

Total Time: 30 minutes
Serves: 4
Ingredients

For Tofu

- 1 lb. extra-firm tofu, pressed and cubed
- 1 tablespoon cornstarch
- 1 tablespoon tamari
- For Sauce
- ½ cup water
- 1/3 cup fresh orange juice
- 1 tablespoon honey
- 1 teaspoon orange zest, grated
- 1 teaspoon garlic, minced
- 1 teaspoon fresh ginger, minced
- 2 teaspoons cornstarch
- ¼ teaspoon red pepper flakes, crushed

Directions

1. In a bowl, add the tofu, cornstarch, and tamari and toss to coat well.
2. Set the tofu aside to marinate for at least 15 minutes.
3. Press "Power Button" of Air Fry Oven and turn the dial to select the "Air Fry" mode.
4. Press the Time button and again turn the dial to set the cooking time to 10 minutes.
5. Now push the Temp button and rotate the dial to set the temperature at 390 degrees F.
6. Press "Start/Pause" button to start.
7. When the unit beeps to show that it is preheated, open the lid.
8. Arrange the tofu cubes in greased "Air Fry Basket" and insert in the oven.
9. Flip the tofu cubes once halfway through.
10. Meanwhile, for the sauce: in a small pan, add all the ingredients over medium-high heat and bring to a boil, stirring continuously.
11. Transfer the tofu into a serving bowl with the sauce and gently stir to combine.

12. Serve immediately.

TOFU WITH CAPERS

Total Time: 40 minutes
Serves: 4
Ingredients

For Marinade

- ¼ cup fresh lemon juice
- 2 tablespoons fresh parsley
- 1 garlic clove, peeled
- Salt and ground black pepper, as required

For Tofu

- 1 (14-oz.) block extra-firm tofu, pressed and cut into 8 rectangular cutlets
- ½ cup mayonnaise
- 1 cup panko breadcrumbs

For Sauce

- 1 cup vegetable broth
- ¼ cup lemon juice
- 1 garlic clove, peeled
- 2 tablespoons fresh parsley
- 2 teaspoons cornstarch
- Salt and ground black pepper, as required
- 2 tablespoons capers

Directions

1. For marinade: in a food processor, add all the ingredients and pulse until smooth.
2. In a bowl, mix together the marinade and tofu.
3. Set aside for about 15-30 minutes.
4. In 2 shallow bowls, place the mayonnaise and panko breadcrumbs respectively.
5. Coat the tofu pieces with mayonnaise and then, roll into the panko.
6. Press "Power Button" of Air Fry Oven and turn the dial to select the "Air Fry" mode.
7. Press the Time button and again turn the dial to set the cooking time to 20 minutes.
8. Now push the Temp button and rotate the dial to set the temperature at 375 degrees F.

9. Press "Start/Pause" button to start.
10. When the unit beeps to show that it is preheated, open the lid.
11. Arrange the tofu cubes in greased "Air Fry Basket" and insert in the oven.
12. Flip the tofu cubes once halfway through.
13. Meanwhile, for the sauce: add broth, lemon juice, garlic, parsley, cornstarch, salt and black pepper in a food processor and pulse until smooth.
14. Transfer the sauce into a small pan and stir in the capers.
15. Place the pan over medium heat and bring to a boil.
16. Reduce the heat to low and simmer for about 5-7 minutes, stirring continuously.
17. Transfer the tofu cubes onto serving plates.
18. Top with the sauce and serve.

TOFU IN SWEET & SOUR SAUCE

Total Time: 40 minutes
Serves: 4
Ingredients

For Tofu

- 1 (14-oz.) block firm tofu, pressed and cubed
- ½ cup arrowroot flour
- ½ teaspoon sesame oil

For Sauce

- 4 tablespoons low-sodium soy sauce
- 1½ tablespoons rice vinegar
- 1½ tablespoons chili sauce
- 1 tablespoon agave nectar
- 2 large garlic cloves, minced
- 1 teaspoon fresh ginger, peeled and grated

- 2 scallions (green part), chopped

Directions

1. In a bowl, mix together the tofu, arrowroot flour, and sesame oil.
2. Press "Power Button" of Air Fry Oven and turn the dial to select the "Air Fry" mode.
3. Press the Time button and again turn the dial to set the cooking time to 20 minutes.
4. Now push the Temp button and rotate the dial to set the temperature at 360 degrees F.
5. Press "Start/Pause" button to start.
6. When the unit beeps to show that it is preheated, open the lid.
7. Arrange the tofu cubes in greased "Air Fry Basket" and insert in the oven.
8. Flip the tofu cubes once halfway through.
9. Meanwhile, for the sauce: in a bowl, add all the ingredients except scallions and beat until well combined.
10. Transfer the tofu into a skillet with sauce over medium heat and cook for about 3 minutes, stirring occasionally.
11. Garnish with scallions and serve hot.

TOFU WITH CAULIFLOWER

Total Time: 30 minutes
Serves: 2
Ingredients
- ½ (14-oz.) block firm tofu, pressed and cubed
- ½ small head cauliflower, cut into florets
- 1 tablespoon canola oil
- 1 tablespoon nutritional yeast
- ¼ teaspoon dried parsley
- 1 teaspoon ground turmeric
- ¼ teaspoon paprika
- Salt and ground black pepper, as required

Directions

1. In a bowl, mix together the tofu, cauliflower and the remaining ingredients.

2. Press "Power Button" of Air Fry Oven and turn the dial to select the "Air Fry" mode.
3. Press the Time button and again turn the dial to set the cooking time to 15 minutes.
4. Now push the Temp button and rotate the dial to set the temperature at 390 degrees F.
5. Press "Start/Pause" button to start.
6. When the unit beeps to show that it is preheated, open the lid.
7. Arrange the tofu mixture in greased "Air Fry Basket" and insert in the oven.
8. Flip the tofu mixture once halfway through.
9. Serve hot.

SPAGHETTI SQUASH LASAGNA

Total Time: 35

Serves: 4

Ingredients
- 3 lb. spaghetti squash, halved lengthwise & seeded
- 4 tbsp. water, divided
- 1 tbsp. extra-virgin olive oil
- 1 bunch broccolini, chopped
- 4 cloves garlic, chopped fine
- ¼ tsp crushed red pepper flakes
- 1 cup mozzarella cheese, grated &divided
- ¼ cup parmesan cheese, grated & divided
- ¾ tsp Italian seasoning
- ½ tsp salt
- ¼ tsp ground pepper

Directions
1. Place squash, cut side down, in a microwave safe dish. Add 2 tablespoons water and microwave on high until tender, about 10 minutes.
2. Heat oil in a large skillet over medium heat. Add broccoli, garlic, and red pepper. Cook, stirring frequently, 2 minutes.
3. Add remaining water and cook until broccolini is tender, about 3-5 minutes. Transfer to a large bowl.
4. With a fork, scrape the squash from the shells into the bowl with the broccolini. Place the shells in an 8x11-inch baking pan.

5. Add ¾ cup mozzarella, 2 tablespoons parmesan, and seasonings to the squash mixture and stir to combine. Spoon evenly into the shells and top with remaining cheese.
6. Place rack in position 1 and set oven to bake on 450°F for 15 minutes. After 5 minutes, place the squash in the oven and cook 10 minutes.
7. Set the oven to broil on high and move the pan to position 2. Broil until cheese starts to brown, about 2 minutes. Serve immediately.

GREEN CHILI TAQUITOS

Total Time: 15 minutes

Serves: 3

Ingredients
- Nonstick cooking spray
- 6 corn tortillas
- ¾ cup vegan cream cheese
- 1 cup vegan cheddar cheese, grated
- 4 oz. green chilies, diced & drained

Directions
1. Place baking pan in position 2. Lightly spray fryer basket with cooking spray.
2. Wrap tortillas in paper towels and microwave 1 minute.
3. Spread the cream cheese over tortillas. Top with cheddar cheese and chilies. Roll up tightly. Place, seam side down, in fryer basket.
4. Place the basket on the baking pan and set oven to air fry on 350°F for 10 minutes or until tortillas are browned and crispy. Turn taquitos over halfway through cooking time. Serve immediately.

CHICKPEA FRITTERS

Total Time: 15 minutes

Serves: 4

Ingredients
- Nonstick cooking spray
- 1 cup chickpeas, cooked
- 1 onion, chopped
- ¼ tsp salt
- ¼ tsp pepper
- ¼ tsp turmeric
- ¼ tsp coriander

Directions
1. Place the baking pan in position 2. Lightly spray the fryer basket with cooking spray.
2. Add the onion to a food processor and pulse until finely diced.
3. Add remaining ingredients and pulse until combined but not pureed.
4. Form the mixture into 8 patties and place them in the fryer basket, these may need to be cooked in two batches.
5. Place the basket in the oven and set to air fry on 350°F for 10 minutes. Cook fritters until golden brown and crispy, turning over halfway through cooking time. Serve with your favorite dipping sauce.

ROASTEd FALL VEGGIES

Total Time: 40 minutes

Serves: 6

Ingredients
- 2 cups sweet potatoes, cubed
- 2 cups Brussel sprouts, halved
- 3 cups button mushrooms, halved
- ½ red onion, chopped
- 3 cloves garlic, chopped fine
- 4 sage leaves, chopped
- 2 sprigs rosemary, chopped
- 2 sprigs thyme, chopped
- 1 tsp garlic powder
- 1 tsp onion powder

- ½ tsp salt
- ¼ tsp pepper
- 3 tbsp. balsamic vinegar
- Nonstick cooking spray

Directions

1. Chop vegetables so that they are as close to equal in size as possible. Roughly chop the herbs.
2. In a large bowl, toss vegetables, herbs, and spices to mix. Drizzle vinegar overall and toss to coat.
3. Spray the baking pan with cooking spray. Set oven to bake on 350°F for 35 minutes.
4. Transfer the vegetable mixture to the baking pan and after 5 minutes, place in the oven in position 1. Bake vegetables 25-30 minutes or until vegetables are tender. Turn them over halfway through cooking. Serve immediately.

ASIAN TOFU "MEATBALLS"

Total Time: 30 minutes

Serves: 4

Ingredients

- 3 dried shitake mushrooms
- Nonstick cooking spray
- 14 oz. firm tofu, drained & pressed
- ¼ cup carrots, cooked
- ¼ cup bamboo shoots, sliced thin
- ½ cup Panko bread crumbs
- 2 tbsp. corn starch
- 3 ½ tablespoon soy sauce, divided
- 1 tsp garlic powder
- ¼ tsp salt
- 1/8 tsp pepper
- 1 tbsp. olive oil
- 2 tbsp. garlic, diced fine
- 2 tbsp. ketchup

- 2 tsp sugar

Directions

1. Place the shitake mushrooms in a bowl and add just enough water to cover. Let soak 20 minutes until soft. Drain well and chop.
2. Place the baking pan in position 2. Lightly spray the fryer basket with cooking spray.
3. Place mushrooms, tofu, carrots, bamboo shoots, bread crumbs, corn starch, 1 ½ tablespoons soy sauce, and seasonings in a food processor. Pulse until thoroughly combined. Form mixture into 1-inch balls.
4. Place balls in fryer basket, these may need to be cooked in batches, and place in oven. Set to air fry on 380°F for 10 minutes. Turn the balls around halfway through cooking time.
5. Heat oil in a saucepan over medium heat. Add garlic and cook 1 minute.
6. Stir in remaining soy sauce, ketchup, and sugar. Bring to a simmer and cook until sauce thickens, 3-5 minutes.
7. When the meatballs are done, add them to sauce and stir to coat. Serve immediately.

FISH AND SEAFOOD RECIPES

SHRIMP IN LEMON SAUCE

Total Time: 18 minutes
Serves: 4
Ingredients
- 1 1/4 lbs. large shrimp, peeled and deveined
- Cooking spray
- 1/4 cup fresh lemon juice
- 2 tablespoons light butter, melted
- 3 garlic cloves, minced
- 1 teaspoon Worcestershire sauce
- 3/4 teaspoon lemon-pepper seasoning
- 1/4 teaspoon ground red pepper
- 2 tablespoons chopped fresh parsley

Directions
1. Toss the shrimp with oil and all other ingredients in a bowl.
2. Spread the seasoned shrimp in the baking tray.
3. Press "Power Button" of Air Fry Oven and turn the dial to select the "Air Roast" mode.
4. Press the Time button and again turn the dial to set the cooking time to 8 minutes.
5. Now push the Temp button and rotate the dial to set the temperature at 425 degrees F.
6. Once preheated, place the shrimp's baking tray in the oven and close its lid.
7. Serve warm.

GARLIC SHRIMP SKEWERS

Total Time: 18 minutes
Serves: 8
Ingredients
- 1 lb. prawns, peeled and deveined

- 2 tablespoons olive oil
- Salt, to taste
- 3 tablespoons butter
- 3 garlic cloves, minced
- 1/4 teaspoon salt
- 1 teaspoon minced chives for garnish

Directions
1. Toss the shrimp with oil and all other ingredients in a bowl.
2. Spread the seasoned shrimp in the baking tray.
3. Press "Power Button" of Air Fry Oven and turn the dial to select the "Air Roast" mode.
4. Press the Time button and again turn the dial to set the cooking time to 8 minutes.
5. Now push the Temp button and rotate the dial to set the temperature at 425 degrees F.
6. Once preheated, place the shrimp's baking tray in the oven and close its lid.
7. Serve warm.

SHRIMP SKEWERS WITH PINEAPPLE

Total Time: 16 minutes
Serves: 4
Ingredients
- 1/2 cup coconut milk
- 4 teaspoons Tabasco Sauce
- 2 teaspoons soy sauce
- 1/4 cup orange juice
- 1/4 cup lime juice
- 1 lb. shrimp, peeled and deveined
- 3/4 lb. pineapple chunks, diced

Directions
1. Toss the shrimp and pineapple with all other ingredients in a bowl.
2. Thread shrimp and pineapple on the skewers.
3. Place the shrimp pineapple skewers in the Air fryer Basket.
4. Press "Power Button" of Air Fry Oven and turn the dial to select the "Air fry" mode.
5. Press the Time button and again turn the dial to set the cooking time to 6 minutes.

6. Now push the Temp button and rotate the dial to set the temperature at 350 degrees F.
7. Once preheated, place the Air fryer basket in the oven and close its lid.
8. Toss and flip the shrimp when cooked halfway through.
9. Serve warm.

TERIYAKI SHRIMP SKEWER

Total Time: 16 minutes
Serves: 4
Ingredients

Shrimp Skewers:

- 1 lb. shrimp, peeled and deveined
- 1 pineapple, peeled, and cut into chunks
- 2 zucchinis, cut into thick slices
- 3 red and orange bell peppers, cut into 2-inch chunks
- Bamboo or metal skewers

Teriyaki BBQ Sauce:

- 1/2 cup teriyaki sauce
- 2 tablespoon fish sauce
- 2 tablespoon chili garlic sauce

Directions
1. Toss the shrimp and veggies with all other ingredients in a bowl.
2. Thread shrimp and veggies on the skewers alternately.
3. Place the shrimp vegetable skewers in the Air fryer Basket.
4. Mix the teriyaki sauce ingredients in a bowl and pour over the skewers.
5. Press "Power Button" of Air Fry Oven and turn the dial to select the "Air fry" mode.
6. Press the Time button and again turn the dial to set the cooking time to 6 minutes.
7. Now push the Temp button and rotate the dial to set the temperature at 350 degrees F.
8. Once preheated, place the Air fryer basket in the oven and close its lid.
9. Toss and flip the shrimp when cooked halfway through.
10. Serve warm.

CAJUN SHRIMP SKEWERS

Total Time: 16 minutes
Serves: 8
Ingredients
- 1/2 cup 8 tablespoon butter
- 4 cloves of garlic pressed or minced
- 1 tablespoon Cajun spice
- 1/2 teaspoon salt
- 1 tablespoon lemon juice
- 2 lbs. shrimp, peeled and deveined

Directions
1. Toss the shrimp and garlic with all other ingredients in a bowl.
2. Thread shrimp on the skewers.
3. Place the shrimp skewers in the Air fryer Basket.
4. Press "Power Button" of Air Fry Oven and turn the dial to select the "Air fry" mode.
5. Press the Time button and again turn the dial to set the cooking time to 6 minutes.
6. Now push the Temp button and rotate the dial to set the temperature at 350 degrees F.
7. Once preheated, place the Air fryer basket in the oven and close its lid.
8. Toss and flip the shrimp when cooked halfway through.
9. Serve warm.

ITALIAN SHRIMP SKEWERS

Total Time: 16 minutes
Serves: 4
Ingredients
- 1 lb. large shrimp peeled and deveined
- 1/4 cup olive oil
- 2 tablespoons lemon juice
- 3/4 teaspoon salt
- 1/4 teaspoon pepper
- 1 teaspoon Italian seasoning
- 2 teaspoons garlic minced

- 1 tablespoon parsley chopped
- lemon wedges for serving

Directions
1. Toss the shrimp with all other ingredients in a bowl.
2. Thread shrimp on the skewers.
3. Place the shrimp skewers in the Air fryer Basket.
4. Press "Power Button" of Air Fry Oven and turn the dial to select the "Air fry" mode.
5. Press the Time button and again turn the dial to set the cooking time to 6 minutes.
6. Now push the Temp button and rotate the dial to set the temperature at 350 degrees F.
7. Once preheated, place the Air fryer basket in the oven and close its lid.
8. Toss and flip the shrimp when cooked halfway through.
9. Serve warm.

PRAWN BURGERS

Total Time: 21 minutes
Serves: 2
Ingredients
- ½ cup prawns, peeled, deveined and chopped very finely
- ½ cup breadcrumbs
- 2-3 tablespoons onion, chopped finely
- ½ teaspoon ginger, minced
- ½ teaspoon garlic, minced
- ½ teaspoon red chili powder
- ½ teaspoon ground cumin
- ¼ teaspoon ground turmeric
- Salt and ground black pepper, as required

Directions
1. In a bowl, add all ingredients and mix until well combined.
2. Make small sized patties from mixture.
3. Press "Power Button" of Air Fry Oven and turn the dial to select the "Air Fry" mode.
4. Press the Time button and again turn the dial to set the cooking time to 6 minutes.
5. Now push the Temp button and rotate the dial to set the temperature at 355 degrees F.

6. Press "Start/Pause" button to start.
7. When the unit beeps to show that it is preheated, open the lid.
8. Arrange the patties in greased "Air Fry Basket" and insert in the oven.
9. Serve hot.

BANG BANG BREAdEd SHRIMP

Total Time: 24 minutes
Serves: 4
Ingredients
- 1 lb. raw shrimp peeled and deveined
- 1 egg white
- 1/2 cup flour
- 3/4 cup panko bread crumbs
- 1 teaspoon paprika
- Montreal Seasoning to taste
- salt and pepper to taste
- cooking spray

Bang Bang Sauce

- 1/3 cup Greek yogurt
- 2 tablespoon Sriracha
- 1/4 cup sweet chili sauce

Directions
1. Mix flour with salt, black pepper, paprika, and Montreal seasoning in a bowl.
2. Dredge the shrimp the flour then dip in the egg.
3. Coat the shrimp with the breadcrumbs and place them in an Air fryer basket.
4. Press "Power Button" of Air Fry Oven and turn the dial to select the "Air Roast" mode.
5. Press the Time button and again turn the dial to set the cooking time to 14 minutes.
6. Now push the Temp button and rotate the dial to set the temperature at 400 degrees F.
7. Once preheated, place the Air fryer basket in the oven and close its lid.
8. Toss and flip the shrimp when cooked halfway through.
9. Serve warm.

TACO FRIED SHRIMP

Total Time: 15 minutes
Serves: 6
Ingredients
- 17 shrimp, defrosted, peeled, and deveined
- 1 cup bread crumbs Italian
- 1 tablespoon taco seasoning
- 1 tablespoon garlic salt
- 4 tablespoon butter melted
- olive oil spray

Directions
1. Toss the shrimp with oil and all other ingredients in a bowl.
2. Spread the seasoned shrimp in the Air fryer Basket.
3. Press "Power Button" of Air Fry Oven and turn the dial to select the "Air Roast" mode.
4. Press the Time button and again turn the dial to set the cooking time to 5 minutes.
5. Now push the Temp button and rotate the dial to set the temperature at 400 degrees F.
6. Once preheated, place the Air fryer basket in the oven and close its lid.
7. Toss and flip the shrimp when cooked halfway through.
8. Serve warm.

GARLIC MUSSELS

Total Time: 16 minutes
Serves: 4
Ingredients
- 1 lb. mussels
- 1 tablespoon butter
- 1 cup of water
- 2 teaspoons minced garlic
- 1 teaspoon chives
- 1 teaspoon basil
- 1 teaspoon parsley

Directions

1. Toss the mussels with oil and all other ingredients in a bowl.
2. Spread the seasoned shrimp in the oven baking tray.
3. Press "Power Button" of Air Fry Oven and turn the dial to select the "Air Roast" mode.
4. Press the Time button and again turn the dial to set the cooking time to 6 minutes.
5. Now push the Temp button and rotate the dial to set the temperature at 390 degrees F.
6. Once preheated, place the mussel's tray in the oven and close its lid.
7. Serve warm.

MUSSELS WITH SAFFRON SAUCE

Total Time: 18 minutes
Serves: 4
Ingredients
- 1 tablespoon unsalted butter
- 1 tablespoon minced garlic
- 1 tablespoon minced shallot
- 1/4 cup dry white wine
- 3 tablespoons heavy cream
- 4 threads saffron
- 1 lb. fresh mussels

Directions
1. Whisk cream with saffron, shallots, white wine, and butter in a bowl.
2. Place the mussels in the oven baking tray and pour the cream sauce on top.
3. Press "Power Button" of Air Fry Oven and turn the dial to select the "Bake" mode.
4. Press the Time button and again turn the dial to set the cooking time to 8 minutes.
5. Now push the Temp button and rotate the dial to set the temperature at 370 degrees F.
6. Once preheated, place the mussel's baking tray in the oven and close its lid.
7. Serve warm.

CAJUN SHRIMP BAKE

Total Time: 50 minutes
Serves: 8
Ingredients
- 4 andouille sausages, chopped
- 1 lb. shrimp, peeled and deveined
- 4 red potatoes, quartered
- 2 pieces corn, quartered
- 2 tablespoons oil, divided
- 1 tablespoon butter, cubed
- 4 cloves garlic, minced

Cajun Spice Mix

- 2 teaspoons garlic powder
- 2 ½ teaspoons paprika
- 1 ¼ teaspoons dried oregano
- 1 teaspoon onion powder
- 1 ¼ teaspoons dried thyme
- ½ teaspoon red pepper flakes
- 1 teaspoon cayenne pepper
- 2 teaspoons salt
- 1 teaspoon pepper

Directions
1. Mix Cajun mix spices in a bowl and then toss in all the veggies and seafood.
2. Stir in sausage, corn, oil, and butter then mix well.
3. Spread potatoes, corn, and garlic in the oven baking tray.
4. Press "Power Button" of Air Fry Oven and turn the dial to select the "Bake" mode.
5. Press the Time button and again turn the dial to set the cooking time to 25 minutes.
6. Now push the Temp button and rotate the dial to set the temperature at 375 degrees F.
7. Once preheated, place the potato's baking tray in the oven and close its lid.
8. When potatoes are done, add shrimp and sausage to the potatoes.
9. Return the baking tray to the oven and bake for 15 minutes.
10. Serve warm.

SHRIMP WITH GARLIC SAUCE

Total Time: 23 minutes
Serves: 4
Ingredients
- 1 1/4 lbs. shrimp, peeled and deveined
- 1/4 cup butter
- 1 tablespoon minced garlic
- 2 tablespoon fresh lemon juice
- Salt and pepper
- 1/8 teaspoon Red pepper flakes
- 2 tablespoon minced fresh parsley

Directions
1. Toss the shrimp with oil and all other ingredients in a bowl.
2. Spread the seasoned shrimp in the baking pan.
3. Press "Power Button" of Air Fry Oven and turn the dial to select the "Bake" mode.
4. Press the Time button and again turn the dial to set the cooking time to 13 minutes.
5. Now push the Temp button and rotate the dial to set the temperature at 350 degrees F.
6. Once preheated, place the baking pan in the oven and close its lid.
7. Serve warm.

SHRIMP SCAMPI

Total Time: 23 minutes
Serves: 8
Ingredients
- 2 lbs. jumbo shrimp, deveined and peeled
- 3 tablespoons olive oil
- 4 tablespoons lemon juice
- 2 teaspoons salt
- 1/2 teaspoon black pepper
- 1/4 cup butter
- 4 cloves garlic, minced
- 1 small shallot, minced

- 2 tablespoons minced fresh parsley
- 1/2 teaspoon dried oregano
- 1/4 teaspoon crushed red pepper flakes
- 1 egg yolk
- 2/3 cup panko bread crumbs

Directions
1. Toss shrimp with egg, spices, seasonings, oil, herbs, butter, and shallots in a bowl.
2. Mix well, then add breadcrumbs to coat well.
3. Spread the shrimp in a baking tray in a single layer.
4. Press "Power Button" of Air Fry Oven and turn the dial to select the "Bake" mode.
5. Press the Time button and again turn the dial to set the cooking time to 13 minutes.
6. Now push the Temp button and rotate the dial to set the temperature at 425 degrees F.
7. Once preheated, place the shrimp's baking tray in the oven and close its lid.
8. Toss and flip the shrimp when cooked halfway through.
9. Serve warm.

SHRIMP PARMESAN BAKE

Total Time: 18 minutes
Serves: 4
Ingredients
- 1 1/2 lb. large raw shrimp, peeled and deveined
- 1/4 cup melted butter
- 1 teaspoon coarse salt
- 1/4 teaspoon black pepper
- 1 teaspoon garlic powder
- 1/2 teaspoon crushed red pepper
- 1/4 cup Parmesan cheese, grated

Directions
1. Toss the shrimp with oil and all other ingredients in a bowl.
2. Spread the seasoned shrimp in the Baking tray.
3. Press "Power Button" of Air Fry Oven and turn the dial to select the "Bake" mode.
4. Press the Time button and again turn the dial to set the cooking time to 8 minutes.

5. Now push the Temp button and rotate the dial to set the temperature at 400 degrees F.
6. Once preheated, place the lobster's baking tray in the oven and close its lid.
7. Switch the Air fryer oven to broil mode and cook for 1 minute.
8. Serve warm.

SHRIMP IN LEMON SAUCE

Total Time: 18 minutes
Serves: 4
Ingredients
- 1 1/4 lbs. large shrimp, peeled and deveined
- Cooking spray
- 1/4 cup fresh lemon juice
- 2 tablespoons light butter, melted
- 3 garlic cloves, minced
- 1 teaspoon Worcestershire sauce
- 3/4 teaspoon lemon-pepper seasoning
- 1/4 teaspoon ground red pepper
- 2 tablespoons chopped fresh parsley

Directions
1. Toss the shrimp with oil and all other ingredients in a bowl.
2. Spread the seasoned shrimp in the baking tray.
3. Press "Power Button" of Air Fry Oven and turn the dial to select the "Air Roast" mode.
4. Press the Time button and again turn the dial to set the cooking time to 8 minutes.
5. Now push the Temp button and rotate the dial to set the temperature at 425 degrees F.
6. Once preheated, place the shrimp's baking tray in the oven and close its lid.
7. Serve warm.

GARLIC SHRIMP SKEWERS

Total Time: 18 minutes

Serves: 8
Ingredients
- 1 lb. prawns, peeled and deveined
- 2 tablespoons olive oil
- Salt, to taste
- 3 tablespoons butter
- 3 garlic cloves, minced
- 1/4 teaspoon salt
- 1 teaspoon minced chives for garnish

Directions
1. Toss the shrimp with oil and all other ingredients in a bowl.
2. Spread the seasoned shrimp in the baking tray.
3. Press "Power Button" of Air Fry Oven and turn the dial to select the "Air Roast" mode.
4. Press the Time button and again turn the dial to set the cooking time to 8 minutes.
5. Now push the Temp button and rotate the dial to set the temperature at 425 degrees F.
6. Once preheated, place the shrimp's baking tray in the oven and close its lid.
7. Serve warm.

SHRIMP SKEWERS WITH PINEAPPLE

Total Time: 16 minutes
Serves: 4
Ingredients
- 1/2 cup coconut milk
- 4 teaspoons Tabasco Sauce
- 2 teaspoons soy sauce
- 1/4 cup orange juice
- 1/4 cup lime juice
- 1 lb. shrimp, peeled and deveined
- 3/4 lb. pineapple chunks, diced

Directions

1. Toss the shrimp and pineapple with all other ingredients in a bowl.
2. Thread shrimp and pineapple on the skewers.
3. Place the shrimp pineapple skewers in the Air fryer Basket.
4. Press "Power Button" of Air Fry Oven and turn the dial to select the "Air fry" mode.
5. Press the Time button and again turn the dial to set the cooking time to 6 minutes.
6. Now push the Temp button and rotate the dial to set the temperature at 350 degrees F.
7. Once preheated, place the Air fryer basket in the oven and close its lid.
8. Toss and flip the shrimp when cooked halfway through.
9. Serve warm.

TERIYAKI SHRIMP SKEWER

Total Time: 16 minutes
Serves: 4
Ingredients

Shrimp Skewers:

- 1 lb. shrimp, peeled and deveined
- 1 pineapple, peeled, and cut into chunks
- 2 zucchinis, cut into thick slices
- 3 red and orange bell peppers, cut into 2-inch chunks
- Bamboo or metal skewers

Teriyaki BBQ Sauce:

- 1/2 cup teriyaki sauce
- 2 tablespoon fish sauce
- 2 tablespoon chili garlic sauce

Directions

1. Toss the shrimp and veggies with all other ingredients in a bowl.
2. Thread shrimp and veggies on the skewers alternately.
3. Place the shrimp vegetable skewers in the Air fryer Basket.
4. Mix the teriyaki sauce ingredients in a bowl and pour over the skewers.
5. Press "Power Button" of Air Fry Oven and turn the dial to select the "Air fry" mode.

6. Press the Time button and again turn the dial to set the cooking time to 6 minutes.
7. Now push the Temp button and rotate the dial to set the temperature at 350 degrees F.
8. Once preheated, place the Air fryer basket in the oven and close its lid.
9. Toss and flip the shrimp when cooked halfway through.
10. Serve warm.

CAJUN SHRIMP SKEWERS

Total Time: 16 minutes
Serves: 8
Ingredients
- 1/2 cup 8 tablespoon butter
- 4 cloves of garlic pressed or minced
- 1 tablespoon Cajun spice
- 1/2 teaspoon salt
- 1 tablespoon lemon juice
- 2 lbs. shrimp, peeled and deveined

Directions
1. Toss the shrimp and garlic with all other ingredients in a bowl.
2. Thread shrimp on the skewers.
3. Place the shrimp skewers in the Air fryer Basket.
4. Press "Power Button" of Air Fry Oven and turn the dial to select the "Air fry" mode.
5. Press the Time button and again turn the dial to set the cooking time to 6 minutes.
6. Now push the Temp button and rotate the dial to set the temperature at 350 degrees F.
7. Once preheated, place the Air fryer basket in the oven and close its lid.
8. Toss and flip the shrimp when cooked halfway through.
9. Serve warm.

ITALIAN SHRIMP SKEWERS

Total Time: 16 minutes
Serves: 4

Ingredients
- 1 lb. large shrimp peeled and deveined
- 1/4 cup olive oil
- 2 tablespoons lemon juice
- 3/4 teaspoon salt
- 1/4 teaspoon pepper
- 1 teaspoon Italian seasoning
- 2 teaspoons garlic minced
- 1 tablespoon parsley chopped
- lemon wedges for serving

Directions
1. Toss the shrimp with all other ingredients in a bowl.
2. Thread shrimp on the skewers.
3. Place the shrimp skewers in the Air fryer Basket.
4. Press "Power Button" of Air Fry Oven and turn the dial to select the "Air fry" mode.
5. Press the Time button and again turn the dial to set the cooking time to 6 minutes.
6. Now push the Temp button and rotate the dial to set the temperature at 350 degrees F.
7. Once preheated, place the Air fryer basket in the oven and close its lid.
8. Toss and flip the shrimp when cooked halfway through.
9. Serve warm.

PRAWN BURGERS

Total Time: 21 minutes
Serves: 2
Ingredients
- ½ cup prawns, peeled, deveined and chopped very finely
- ½ cup breadcrumbs
- 2-3 tablespoons onion, chopped finely
- ½ teaspoon ginger, minced
- ½ teaspoon garlic, minced
- ½ teaspoon red chili powder
- ½ teaspoon ground cumin
- ¼ teaspoon ground turmeric

- Salt and ground black pepper, as required

Directions

1. In a bowl, add all ingredients and mix until well combined.
2. Make small sized patties from mixture.
3. Press "Power Button" of Air Fry Oven and turn the dial to select the "Air Fry" mode.
4. Press the Time button and again turn the dial to set the cooking time to 6 minutes.
5. Now push the Temp button and rotate the dial to set the temperature at 355 degrees F.
6. Press "Start/Pause" button to start.
7. When the unit beeps to show that it is preheated, open the lid.
8. Arrange the patties in greased "Air Fry Basket" and insert in the oven.
9. Serve hot.

PORK WITH QUINOA SALAd

Total Time: 22 minutes
Serves: 4
Ingredients
- 2/3 lbs. lean pork shoulder, cubed
- 1 teaspoon ground cumin
- ½ teaspoon cayenne pepper
- 1 teaspoon sweet smoked paprika
- 1 tablespoon olive oil
- 24 cherry tomatoes

Salad:

- ½ cup quinoa, boiled
- ½ cup frozen pea
- 1 large carrot, grated
- small pack coriander, chopped
- small pack mint, chopped
- juice 1 lemon
- 2 tablespoon olive oil

Directions
1. Toss pork with oil, paprika, pepper, and cumin in a bowl.
2. Alternatively, thread the pork on the skewers.
3. Place these pork skewers in the Air fry basket.
4. Press "Power Button" of Air Fry Oven and turn the dial to select the "Air fryer" mode.
5. Press the Time button and again turn the dial to set the cooking time to 10 minutes.
6. Now push the Temp button and rotate the dial to set the temperature at 370 degrees F.
7. Once preheated, place the Air fryer basket in the oven and close its lid.
8. Flip the skewers when cooked halfway through then resume cooking.
9. Meanwhile, sauté carrots and peas with olive oil in a pan for 2 minutes.
10. Stir in mint, lemon juice, coriander, and cooked quinoa.
11. Serve skewers with the couscous salad.

PORK GARLIC SKEWERS

Total Time: 30 minutes
Serves: 4
Ingredients
- 1 lb. pork, boned and diced
- 1 lemon, juiced and chopped
- 3 tablespoon olive oil
- 20 garlic cloves, chopped
- 1 handful rosemary, chopped
- 3 green peppers, cubed
- 2 red onions, cut into wedges

Directions
1. Toss the pork with the rest of the skewer's ingredients in a bowl.
2. Thread the pork, peppers, garlic, and onion on the skewers, alternately.
3. Place these pork skewers in the Air fry basket.
4. Press "Power Button" of Air Fry Oven and turn the dial to select the "Air fryer" mode.
5. Press the Time button and again turn the dial to set the cooking time to 20 minutes.
6. Now push the Temp button and rotate the dial to set the temperature at 370 degrees F.
7. Once preheated, place the Air fryer basket in the oven and close its lid.
8. Flip the skewers when cooked halfway through then resume cooking.
9. Serve warm.

ZESTY PORK SKEWERS

Total Time: 30 minutes
Serves: 4
Ingredients
- 2 teaspoons ground cumin
- 2 teaspoons ground coriander
- 1 onion, cut into pieces
- 1/4 teaspoon ground cinnamon

- 1/8 teaspoon ground smoked paprika
- 2 teaspoons orange zest
- 1/2 yellow bell pepper, sliced into squares
- 1/2 teaspoon salt
- 1/2 teaspoon black pepper
- 1 tablespoon lemon juice
- 2 teaspoons olive oil
- 1 1/2 lbs. pork, cubed

Directions

1. Toss pork with the rest of the skewer's ingredients in a bowl.
2. Thread the pork and veggies on the skewers alternately.
3. Place these pork skewers in the Air fry basket.
4. Press "Power Button" of Air Fry Oven and turn the dial to select the "Air fryer" mode.
5. Press the Time button and again turn the dial to set the cooking time to 20 minutes.
6. Now push the Temp button and rotate the dial to set the temperature at 370 degrees F.
7. Once preheated, place the Air fryer basket in the oven and close its lid.
8. Flip the skewers when cooked halfway through then resume cooking.
9. Serve warm.

ALEPO PORK KEBOBS

Total Time: 26 minutes
Serves: 6
Ingredients

Pork Kabobs

- 1 lb. ground pork
- 1/2 an onion, finely diced
- 3 garlic cloves, finely minced
- 2 teaspoons cumin
- 2 teaspoons coriander
- 2 teaspoons sumac
- 1 teaspoon Aleppo Chili flakes
- 1 ½ teaspoons salt

- 2 tablespoons chopped mint

Directions
1. Toss pork with the rest of the kebob ingredients in a bowl.
2. Make 6 sausages out of this mince and thread them on the skewers.
3. Place these pork skewers in the Air fry basket.
4. Press "Power Button" of Air Fry Oven and turn the dial to select the "Air fryer" mode.
5. Press the Time button and again turn the dial to set the cooking time to 16 minutes.
6. Now push the Temp button and rotate the dial to set the temperature at 370 degrees F.
7. Once preheated, place the Air fryer basket in the oven and close its lid.
8. Flip the skewers when cooked halfway through then resume cooking.
9. Serve the skewers with yogurt sauce.

ZUCCHINI PORK KEBOBS

Total Time: 30 minutes
Serves: 4
Ingredients
- 2 garlic cloves
- 1 teaspoon dried oregano
- olive oil
- 4 pork steaks, diced
- 2 zucchinis, cubed
- 8 fresh bay leaves
- 2 lime, juiced
- a few sprigs parsley, chopped

Directions
1. Toss pork with the rest of the skewer's ingredients in a bowl.
2. Thread the pork and veggies on the skewers alternately.
3. Place these pork skewers in the Air fry basket.
4. Press "Power Button" of Air Fry Oven and turn the dial to select the "Air fryer" mode.
5. Press the Time button and again turn the dial to set the cooking time to 20 minutes.

6. Now push the Temp button and rotate the dial to set the temperature at 370 degrees F.
7. Once preheated, place the Air fryer basket in the oven and close its lid.
8. Flip the skewers when cooked halfway through then resume cooking.
9. Serve warm.

LIME GLAZEd PORK KEBOBS

Total Time: 30 minutes
Serves: 6
Ingredients

- 2 lb. pork, cubed
- 1/2 cup olive oil
- 1 lime juice
- 3 cloves garlic, minced
- 1 onion, sliced
- 1 teaspoon oregano, dried
- 1/4 teaspoon dried thyme,
- 1 teaspoon salt
- 1/4 teaspoon black pepper
- 1 tablespoon parsley, chopped
- 2 red pepper, cut into square
- 1 onion, cut into chunks

Directions

1. Toss pork with the rest of the kebab ingredients in a bowl.
2. Cover the pork and marinate it for 30 minutes.
3. Thread the pork and veggies on the skewers alternately.
4. Place these pork skewers in the Air fry basket.
5. Press "Power Button" of Air Fry Oven and turn the dial to select the "Air fryer" mode.
6. Press the Time button and again turn the dial to set the cooking time to 20 minutes.
7. Now push the Temp button and rotate the dial to set the temperature at 370 degrees F.
8. Once preheated, place the Air fryer basket in the oven and close its lid.
9. Flip the skewers when cooked halfway through then resume cooking.
10. Serve warm.

PORK KEBAB TACOS

Total Time: 30 minutes
Serves: 6
Ingredients
- Pork Kebabs
- 2 lbs. pork loin chops, diced
- 1 large onion, squares
- Salt, to taste

For the Wrap

- 6 burrito wraps
- 1/4 cup onions, sliced
- 1/2 cup tomatoes, sliced
- 1 1/2 cups romaine lettuce, chopped

Directions
1. Toss pork and onion with salt in a bowl to season them.
2. Thread the pork and onion on the skewers alternately.
3. Place these pork skewers in the Air fry basket.
4. Press "Power Button" of Air Fry Oven and turn the dial to select the "Air fryer" mode.
5. Press the Time button and again turn the dial to set the cooking time to 20 minutes.
6. Now push the Temp button and rotate the dial to set the temperature at 370 degrees F.
7. Once preheated, place the Air fryer basket in the oven and close its lid.
8. Flip the skewers when cooked halfway through then resume cooking.
9. Place the warm burrito wrap on the serving plates.
10. Divide the tortilla ingredients on the tortillas and top them with pork kebabs.
11. Serve warm.

RAINBOW PORK SKEWERS

Total Time: 25 minutes
Serves: 4

Ingredients
- 1-lb. boneless pork steaks, diced
- 1 eggplant, diced
- 1 yellow squash, diced
- 1 zucchini, diced
- 1/2 onion
- 4 slices ginger
- 5 cloves garlic
- 1 teaspoon cinnamon, ground
- 1 teaspoon cayenne
- 1 teaspoon salt

Directions
1. Blend all the spices, ginger, garlic, and onion in a blender.
2. Toss the pork and veggies with prepared spice mixture then thread them over the skewers.
3. Marinate the spiced skewers for 30 minutes.
4. Place these pork skewers in the Air fry basket.
5. Press "Power Button" of Air Fry Oven and turn the dial to select the "Air fryer" mode.
6. Press the Time button and again turn the dial to set the cooking time to 15 minutes.
7. Now push the Temp button and rotate the dial to set the temperature at 350 degrees F.
8. Once preheated, place the Air fryer basket in the oven and close its lid.
9. Flip the skewers when cooked halfway through then resume cooking.
10. Serve warm.

TANGY PORK SAUSAGES

Total Time: 28 minutes
Serves: 4
Ingredients
- ¾ lb. ground pork
- ¼ cup breadcrumbs
- ½ cup egg, beaten
- 1 teaspoon cumin
- 1 teaspoon paprika
- 1 teaspoon garlic powder
- 1 teaspoon onion powder
- ½ teaspoon cinnamon
- ½ teaspoon turmeric
- ½ teaspoon fennel seeds

- ½ teaspoon coriander seed, ground
- ½ teaspoon salt

Directions
1. Mix pork mince with all the spices and kebab ingredients in a bowl.
2. Make 4 sausages out of this mixture and thread them on the skewers.
3. Refrigerate the pork skewers for 10 minutes to marinate.
4. Place these pork skewers in the Air fry basket.
5. Press "Power Button" of Air Fry Oven and turn the dial to select the "Air fryer" mode.
6. Press the Time button and again turn the dial to set the cooking time to 8 minutes.
7. Now push the Temp button and rotate the dial to set the temperature at 350 degrees F.
8. Once preheated, place the Air fryer basket in the oven and close its lid.
9. Flip the skewers when cooked halfway through then resume cooking.
10. Serve warm.

ROASTEd PORK SHOULdER

Total Time: 100 minutes
Serves: 12
Ingredients
- 6 lb. pork shoulder, boneless
- 8 cups buttermilk

Spice rub:

- 1 cup olive oil
- juice of 1 lemon
- 1 teaspoon thyme
- 5 teaspoon minced garlic
- Salt to taste
- Black pepper to taste

Directions
1. Soak the pork shoulder in the buttermilk in a pot and cover to marinate.
2. Refrigerate the pork leg for 8 hours then remove it from the milk.
3. Place the pork shoulder in a baking tray.
4. Whisk spice rub ingredients in a bowl and brush over the pork liberally.
5. Press "Power Button" of Air Fry Oven and turn the dial to select the "Air Roast" mode.
6. Press the Time button and again turn the dial to set the cooking time to 1 hr. 30 minutes.
7. Now push the Temp button and rotate the dial to set the temperature at 370 degrees F.
8. Once preheated, place the pork baking tray in the oven and close its lid.
9. Serve warm.

SALMON BURGERS

Total Time: 20 minutes

Serves: 4

Ingredients
- 14.75 oz. can salmon, drain & flake
- ¼ cup onion, chopped fine
- 1 egg
- ¼ cup multi-grain crackers, crushed
- 2 tsp fresh dill, chopped
- ¼ tsp pepper
- Nonstick cooking spray

Directions
1. In a medium bowl, combine all ingredients until combined. Form into 4 patties.
2. Lightly spray fryer basket with cooking spray. Place the baking pan in position 2 of the oven.
3. Set oven to air fryer on 350°F.
4. Place the patties in the basket and set on baking pan. Set timer for 8 minutes. Cook until burgers are golden brown, turning over halfway through cooking time. Serve on toasted buns with choice of toppings.

AIR FRIEd HAddOCK FILETS

Total Time: 30 minutes

Serves: 8

Ingredients
- Nonstick cooking spray
- 2 egg whites
- ½ tsp dill
- ½ tsp pepper
- 1 cup cornflakes, crushed

- 2 lbs. haddock fillets, cut in 8 pieces

Directions

1. Place baking pan in position 2 of the oven. Lightly spray fryer basket with cooking spray.
2. In a shallow bowl, whisk together egg whites, dill, and pepper.
3. Place crushed cornflakes in a separate shallow dish.
4. Dip fish in egg mixture, then cornflakes, coating completely. Place in fryer basket.
5. Place basket on the baking pan and set oven to air fryer on 400°F. Cook 18-20 minutes, turning over halfway through, until fish flakes easily with a fork. Serve.

CRISPY COATEd SCALLOPS

Total Time: 20 minutes

Serves: 4

Ingredients
- Nonstick cooking spray
- 1 lb. sea scallops, patted dry
- 1 teaspoon onion powder
- ½ tsp pepper
- 1 egg
- 1 tbsp. water
- ¼ cup Italian bread crumbs
- Paprika
- 1 tbsp. fresh lemon juice

Directions

1. Lightly spray fryer basket with cooking spray. Place baking pan in position 2 of the oven.
2. Sprinkle scallops with onion powder and pepper.
3. In a shallow dish, whisk together egg and water.
4. Place bread crumbs in a separate shallow dish.
5. Dip scallops in egg then bread crumbs coating them lightly. Place in fryer basket and lightly spray with cooking spray. Sprinkle with paprika.

6. Place the basket on the baking pan and set oven to air fryer on 400°F. Bake 10-12 minutes until scallops are firm on the inside and golden brown on the outside. Drizzle with lemon juice and serve.

TASTY TUNA LOAF

Total Time: 50 minutes

Serves: 6

Ingredients
- Nonstick cooking spray
- 12 oz. can chunk white tuna in water, drain & flake
- ¾ cup bread crumbs
- 1 onion, chopped fine
- 2 eggs, beaten
- ¼ cup milk
- ½ tsp fresh lemon juice
- ½ tsp dill
- 1 tbsp. fresh parsley, chopped
- ½ tsp salt
- ½ tsp pepper

Directions
1. Place rack in position 1 of the oven. Spray a 9-inch loaf pan with cooking spray.
2. In a large bowl, combine all ingredients until thoroughly mixed. Spread evenly in prepared pan.
3. Set oven to bake on 350°F for 45 minutes. After 5 minutes, place the pan in the oven and cook 40 minutes, or until top is golden brown. Slice and serve.

MARYLANd CRAB CAKES

Total Time: 20 minutes

Serves: 6

Ingredients
- Nonstick cooking spray
- 2 eggs
- 1 cup Panko bread crumbs
- 1 stalk celery, chopped
- 3 tbsp. mayonnaise
- 1 tsp Worcestershire sauce
- ¼ cup mozzarella cheese, grated
- 1 tsp Italian seasoning
- 1 tbsp. fresh parsley, chopped
- 1 tsp pepper
- ¾ lb. lump crabmeat, drained

Directions
1. Place baking pan in position 2 of the oven. Lightly spray the fryer basket with cooking spray.
2. In a large bowl, combine all ingredients except crab meat, mix well.
3. Fold in crab carefully so it retains some chunks. Form mixture into 12 patties.
4. Place patties in a single layer in the fryer basket. Place the basket on the baking pan.
5. Set oven to air fryer on 350°F for 10 minutes. Cook until golden brown, turning over halfway through cooking time. Serve immediately.

MEdITERRANEAN SOLE

Total Time: 35 minutes

Serves: 6

Ingredients
- Nonstick cooking spray
- 2 tbsp. olive oil
- 8 scallions, sliced thin
- 2 cloves garlic, diced fine
- 4 tomatoes, chopped
- ½ cup dry white wine
- 2 tbsp. fresh parsley, chopped fine
- 1 tsp oregano
- 1 tsp pepper
- 2 lbs. sole, cut in 6 pieces
- 4 oz. feta cheese, crumbled

Directions
1. Place the rack in position 1 of the oven. Spray an 8x11-inch baking dish with cooking spray.
2. Heat the oil in a medium skillet over medium heat. Add scallions and garlic and cook

until tender, stirring frequently.

3. Add the tomatoes, wine, parsley, oregano, and pepper. Stir to mix. Simmer for 5 minutes, or until sauce thickens. Remove from heat.
4. Pour half the sauce on the bottom of the prepared dish. Lay fish on top then pour remaining sauce over the top. Sprinkle with feta.
5. Set the oven to bake on 400°F for 25 minutes. After 5 minutes, place the baking dish on the rack and cook 15-18 minutes or until fish flakes easily with a fork. Serve immediately.

COCONUT SHRIMP

Total Time: 25 minutes

Serves: 6

Ingredients
- Nonstick cooking spray
- 1/3 cup cornstarch
- ½ tsp cayenne pepper
- 1/8 tsp salt
- 2 egg whites
- 1 tbsp. honey
- 1 tbsp. fresh lime juice
- ½ cup sweetened coconut, chopped fine
- 1 ½ lbs. large shrimp, peel, devein & leave tails on

Directions
1. Place the baking pan in position 2 of the oven. Lightly spray the fryer basket with cooking spray.
2. In a small bowl, combine cornstarch, cayenne pepper, and salt.
3. In a separate small bowl, whisk together egg whites, honey, and lime juice.
4. Place the coconut in a shallow dish.
5. Dredge shrimp in the cornstarch mixture, then egg and finally roll in coconut to coat. Place in a single layer in the basket. Spray lightly with cooking spray.
6. Place basket on the baking pan and set oven to air fry on 425°F for 10 minutes. Cook until shrimp are pink and coconut is lightly toasted. Serve immediately.

SPICY GRILLED HALIBUT

Total Time: 40 minutes

Serves: 4

Ingredients
- ½ cup fresh lemon juice
- 2 jalapeno peppers, seeded & chopped fine
- 4 6 oz. halibut fillets
- Nonstick cooking spray
- ¼ cup cilantro, chopped

Directions
1. In a small bowl, combine lemon juice and chilies, mix well.
2. Place fish in a large Ziploc bag and add marinade. Toss to coat. Refrigerate 30 minutes.
3. Lightly spray the baking pan with cooking spray. Set oven to broil on 400°F for 15 minutes.
4. After 5 minutes, lay fish on the pan and place in position 2 of the oven. Cook 10 minutes, or until fish flakes easily with a fork. Turn fish over and brush with marinade halfway through cooking time.
5. Sprinkle with cilantro before serving.

TROPICAL SHRIMP SKEWERS

Total Time: 20 minutes

Serves: 4

Ingredients
- 1 tbsp. lime juice
- 1 tbsp. honey
- ¼ tsp red pepper flakes
- ¼ tsp pepper
- ¼ tsp ginger

- Nonstick cooking spray
- 1 lb. medium shrimp, peel, devein & leave tails on
- 2 cups peaches, drain & chop
- ½ green bell pepper, chopped fine
- ¼ cup scallions, chopped

Directions

1. Soak 8 small wooden skewers in water for 15 minutes.
2. In a small bowl, whisk together lime juice, honey and spices. Transfer 2 tablespoons of the mixture to a medium bowl.
3. Place the baking pan in position 2 of the oven. Lightly spray fryer basket with cooking spray. Set oven to broil on 400°F for 10 minutes.
4. Thread 5 shrimp on each skewer and brush both sides with marinade. Place in basket and after 5 minutes, place on the baking pan. Cook 4-5 minutes or until shrimp turn pink.
5. Add peaches, bell pepper, and scallions to reserved honey mixture, mix well. Divide salsa evenly between serving plates and top with 2 skewers each. Serve immediately.

SEAFOOd MAC N CHEESE

Total Time: 50 minutes

Serves: 8

Ingredients

- Nonstick cooking spray
- 16 oz. macaroni
- 7 tbsp. butter, divided
- ¾ lb. medium shrimp, peel, devein, & cut in ½-inch pieces
- ½ cup Italian panko bread crumbs
- 1 cup onion, chopped fine
- 1 ½ tsp garlic, diced fine
- 1/3 cup flour
- 3 cups milk
- 1/8 tsp nutmeg
- ½ tsp Old Bay seasoning
- 1 tsp salt
- ¾ tsp pepper

- 1 1/3 cup Parmesan cheese, grated
- 1 1/3 cup Swiss cheese, grated
- 1 1/3 cup sharp cheddar cheese, grated
- ½ lb. lump crab meat, cooked

Directions

1. Place wire rack in position 1 of the oven. Spray a 7x11-inch baking dish with cooking spray.
2. Cook macaroni according to package directions, shortening cooking time by 2 minutes. Drain and rinse with cold water.
3. Melt 1 tablespoon butter in a large skillet over med-high heat. Add shrimp and cook, stirring, until they turn pink. Remove from heat.
4. Melt remaining butter in a large saucepan over medium heat. Once melted, transfer 2 tablespoons to a small bowl and mix in bread crumbs.
5. Add onions and garlic to saucepan and cook, stirring, until they soften.
6. Whisk in flour and cook 1 minute, until smooth.
7. Whisk in milk until there are no lumps. Bring to a boil, reduce heat and simmer until thickened, whisking constantly.
8. Whisk in seasonings. Stir in cheese until melted and smooth. Fold in macaroni and seafood. Transfer to prepared dish. Sprinkle bread crumb mixture evenly over top.
9. Set oven to bake on 400°F for 25 minutes. After 5 minutes, place dish on the rack and bake 20 minutes, until topping is golden brown and sauce is bubbly. Let cool 5 minutes before serving.

SNACKS & APPETIZERS

CHEDDAR BISCUITS

Total Time: 25 minutes
Serves: 8
Ingredients
- 1/3 cup unbleached all-purpose flour
- 1/8 teaspoon cayenne pepper
- 1/8 teaspoon smoked paprika
- Pinch of garlic powder
- Salt and ground black pepper, as required
- ½ cup sharp cheddar cheese, shredded
- 2 tablespoons butter, softened
- Nonstick cooking spray

Directions
1. In a food processor, add the flour, spices, salt and black pepper and pulse until well combined.
2. Add the cheese and butter and pulse until a smooth dough forms.
3. Place the dough onto a lightly floured surface.
4. Make 16 small equal-sized balls from the dough and press each slightly.
5. Press "Power Button" of Air Fry Oven and turn the dial to select the "Air Bake" mode.
6. Press the Time button and again turn the dial to set the cooking time to 10 minutes.
7. Now push the Temp button and rotate the dial to set the temperature at 330 degrees F.
8. Press "Start/Pause" button to start.
9. When the unit beeps to show that it is preheated, open the lid.
10. Arrange the biscuits in greased "Air Fry Basket" and insert in the oven.
11. Place the basket onto a wire rack for about 10 minutes.
12. Carefully, invert the biscuits onto the wire rack to cool completely before serving.

LEMON BISCUITS

Total Time: 20 minutes
Serves: 10
Ingredients
- 8½ oz. self-rising flour
- 3½ oz. caster sugar
- 3½ oz. cold butter
- 1 small egg
- 1 teaspoon fresh lemon zest, grated finely
- 2 tablespoons fresh lemon juice
- 1 teaspoon vanilla extract

Directions
1. In a large bowl, mix together flour and sugar.
2. With a pastry cutter, cut cold butter and mix until a coarse crumb forms.
3. Add the egg, lemon zest and lemon juice and mix until a soft dough forms.
4. Place the dough onto a floured surface and roll the dough.
5. Cut the dough into medium-sized biscuits.
6. Arrange the biscuits into a baking pan in a single layer and coat with the butter.
7. Press "Power Button" of Air Fry Oven and turn the dial to select the "Air Fry" mode.
8. Press the Time button and again turn the dial to set the cooking time to 5 minutes.
9. Now push the Temp button and rotate the dial to set the temperature at 355 degrees F.
10. Press "Start/Pause" button to start.
11. When the unit beeps to show that it is preheated, open the lid.
12. Arrange pan over the "Wire Rack" and insert in the oven.
13. Place the baking pan onto a wire rack for about 10 minutes.
14. Carefully, invert the biscuits onto the wire rack to cool completely before serving.

POTATO BREAd ROLLS

Total Time: 53 minutes
Serves: 8
Ingredients

- 5 large potatoes, peeled
- 2 tablespoons vegetable oil, divided
- 2 small onions, finely chopped
- 2 green chilies, seeded and chopped
- 2 curry leaves
- ½ teaspoon ground turmeric
- Salt, as required
- 8 bread slices, trimmed

Directions
1. In a pan of a boiling water, add the potatoes and cook for about 15-20 minutes.
2. Drain the potatoes well and with a potato masher, mash the potatoes.
3. In a skillet, heat 1 teaspoon of oil over a medium heat and sauté the onion for about 4-5 minutes.
4. Add the green chilies, curry leaves, and turmeric and sauté for about 1 minute.
5. Add the mashed potatoes, and salt and mix well.
6. Remove from the heat and set aside to cool completely.
7. Make 8 equal-sized oval-shaped patties from the mixture.
8. Wet the bread slices completely with water.
9. Press each bread slice between your hands to remove the excess water.
10. Place 1 bread slice in your palm and place 1 patty in the center.
11. Roll the bread slice in a spindle shape and seal the edges to secure the filling.
12. Coat the roll with some oil.
13. Repeat with the remaining slices, filling and oil.
14. Press "Power Button" of Air Fry Oven and turn the dial to select the "Air Fry" mode.
15. Press the Time button and again turn the dial to set the cooking time to 13 minutes.
16. Now push the Temp button and rotate the dial to set the temperature at 390 degrees F.
17. Press "Start/Pause" button to start.
18. When the unit beeps to show that it is preheated, open the lid.
19. Arrange the bread rolls in "Air Fry Basket" and insert in the oven.
20. Serve warm.

VEGGIE SPRING ROLLS

Total Time: 25 minutes
Serves: 6
Ingredients
- 1 tablespoon vegetable oil, divided
- 14 oz. fresh mushrooms, sliced
- ½ oz. canned water chestnuts, sliced
- ½ teaspoon fresh ginger, finely grated
- ½ oz. bean sprouts
- ½ of small carrot, peeled and cut into matchsticks
- 1 scallion (green part), chopped
- ½ tablespoon soy sauce
- ½ teaspoon Chinese five-spice powder
- 1½ oz. cooked shrimps
- 6 spring roll wrappers
- 1 small egg, beaten

Directions
1. In a skillet, heat 1 tablespoon of oil over medium heat and sauté the mushrooms, water chestnuts, and ginger for about 2-3 minutes.
2. Add the beans sprouts, carrot, scallion, soy sauce, and five-spice powder and sauté for about 1 minute.
3. Stir in the shrimps and remove from heat. Set aside to cool.
4. Arrange the spring rolls onto a smooth surface.
5. Divide the veggie mixture evenly between spring rolls.
6. Roll the wrappers around the filling and seal with beaten egg.
7. Coat each roll with the remaining oil.
8. Repeat with the remaining slices, filling and oil.
9. Press "Power Button" of Air Fry Oven and turn the dial to select the "Air Fry" mode.
10. Press the Time button and again turn the dial to set the cooking time to 5 minutes.
11. Now push the Temp button and rotate the dial to set the temperature at 390 degrees F.

12. Press "Start/Pause" button to start.
13. When the unit beeps to show that it is preheated, open the lid.
14. Arrange the rolls in "Air Fry Basket" and insert in the oven.
15. Serve warm.

SPINACH ROLLS

Total Time: 24 minutes
Serves: 6
Ingredients
- 1 red onion, chopped
- 1 cup fresh parsley, chopped
- 1 cup fresh mint leaves, chopped
- 1 egg
- 1 cup feta cheese, crumbled
- ½ cup Romano cheese, grated
- ¼ teaspoon ground cardamom
- Salt and freshly ground black pepper, as needed
- 1 package frozen phyllo dough, thawed
- 1 (16-oz.) package frozen spinach, thawed
- 2 tablespoons olive oil

Directions
1. In a food processor, add all the ingredients except phyllo dough and oil and pulse until smooth.
2. Place one phyllo sheet on the cutting board and cut into three rectangular strips.
3. Brush each strip with the oil.
4. Place about 1 teaspoon of spinach mixture along with the short side of a strip.
5. Roll the dough to secure the filling.
6. Repeat with the remaining phyllo sheets and spinach mixture.
7. Press "Power Button" of Air Fry Oven and turn the dial to select the "Air Fry" mode.
8. Press the Time button and again turn the dial to set the cooking time to 4 minutes.
9. Now push the Temp button and rotate the dial to set the temperature at 355 degrees F.

10. Press "Start/Pause" button to start.

11. When the unit beeps to show that it is preheated, open the lid.

12. Arrange the rolls in "Air Fry Basket" and insert in the oven.
13. Serve warm.

CHEESE PASTRIES

Total Time: 25 minutes
Serves: 6
Ingredients
- 1 egg yolk
- 4 oz. feta cheese, crumbled
- 1 scallion, finely chopped
- 2 tablespoons fresh parsley, finely chopped
- Salt and ground black pepper, as needed
- 2 frozen phyllo pastry sheets, thawed
- 2 tablespoons olive oil

Directions
1. In a large bowl, add the egg yolk, and beat well.
2. Add the feta cheese, scallion, parsley, salt, and black pepper and mix well.
3. Cut each pastry sheet in three strips.
4. Add about 1 teaspoon of feta mixture on the underside of a strip.
5. Fold the tip of sheet over the filling in a zigzag manner to form a triangle.
6. Repeat with the remaining strips and fillings.
7. Coat each pastry with oil evenly.
8. Press "Power Button" of Air Fry Oven and turn the dial to select the "Air Fry" mode.
9. Press the Time button and again turn the dial to set the cooking time to 3 minutes.

10. Now push the Temp button and rotate the dial to set the temperature at 390 degrees F.

11. Press "Start/Pause" button to start.

12. When the unit beeps to show that it is preheated, open the lid.

13. Arrange the pastries in "Air Fry Basket" and insert in the oven.
14. After 3 minutes, set the temperature at 390 degrees F for 2 minutes.
15. Repeat with remaining pastries.
16. Serve warm.

VEGGIE PASTRIES

Total Time: 30 minutes
Serves: 8
Ingredients
- 2 large potatoes, peeled
- 1 tablespoon olive oil
- ½ cup carrot, peeled and chopped
- ½ cup onion, chopped
- 2 garlic cloves, minced
- 2 tablespoons fresh ginger, minced
- ½ cup green peas, shelled
- Salt and ground black pepper, as needed
- 3 puff pastry sheets

Directions
1. In a pan of a boiling water, cook the potatoes for about 15-20 minutes.
2. Drain the potatoes well and with a potato masher, mash the potatoes.
3. In a skillet, heat the oil over medium heat and sauté the carrot, onion, ginger, and garlic for about 4-5 minutes.
4. Drain all the fat from the skillet.
5. Stir in the mashed potatoes, peas, salt, and black pepper and cook for about 1-2 minutes.
6. Remove the potato mixture from heat and set aside to cool completely.
7. Arrange the puff pastry onto a smooth surface.
8. Cut each puff pastry sheet into four pieces and then cut each piece in a round shape.
9. Place about 2 tablespoons of veggie filling over each pastry round.
10. With your wet fingers, moisten the edges.

11. Fold each pastry round in half to seal the filling.
12. With a fork, firmly press the edges.
13. Press "Power Button" of Air Fry Oven and turn the dial to select the "Air Fry" mode.
14. Press the Time button and again turn the dial to set the cooking time to 5 minutes.
15. Now push the Temp button and rotate the dial to set the temperature at 390 degrees F.
16. Press "Start/Pause" button to start.
17. When the unit beeps to show that it is preheated, open the lid.
18. Arrange half of the pastries in "Air Fry Basket" and insert in the oven.
19. Repeat with remaining pastries.
20. Serve warm.

SPINACH DIP

Total Time: 50 minutes
Serves: 8
Ingredients
- 1 (8-oz.) package cream cheese, softened
- 1 cup mayonnaise
- 1 cup Parmesan cheese, grated
- 1 cup frozen spinach, thawed and squeezed
- 1/3 cup water chestnuts, drained and chopped
- ½ cup onion, minced
- ¼ teaspoon garlic powder
- Ground black pepper, as required

Directions
1. In a bowl, add all the ingredients and mix until well combined.
2. Transfer the mixture into a baking pan and spread in an even layer.
3. Press "Power Button" of Air Fry Oven and turn the dial to select the "Air Fry" mode.
4. Press the Time button and again turn the dial to set the cooking time to 35 minutes.
5. Now push the Temp button and rotate the dial to set the temperature at 300 degrees F.

6. Press "Start/Pause" button to start.
7. When the unit beeps to show that it is preheated, open the lid.
8. Arrange pan over the "Wire Rack" and insert in the oven.
9. Stir the dip once halfway through.
10. Serve hot.

CHILI DIP

Total Time: 25 minutes
Serves: 8
Ingredients
- 1 (8-oz.) package cream cheese, softened
- 1 (16-oz.) can Hormel chili without beans
- 1 (16-oz.) package mild cheddar cheese, shredded

Directions
1. In a baking pan, place the cream cheese and spread in an even layer.
2. Top with chili evenly, followed by the cheese.
3. Press "Power Button" of Air Fry Oven and turn the dial to select the "Air Bake" mode.
4. Press the Time button and again turn the dial to set the cooking time to 15 minutes.
5. Now push the Temp button and rotate the dial to set the temperature at 375 degrees F.
6. Press "Start/Pause" button to start.
7. When the unit beeps to show that it is preheated, open the lid.
8. Arrange pan over the "Wire Rack" and insert in the oven.
9. Serve hot.

ONION DIP

Total Time: 55 minutes
Serves: 10
Ingredients
- 2/3 cup onion, chopped

- 1 cup cheddar jack cheese, shredded
- ½ cup Swiss cheese, shredded
- ¼ cup Parmesan cheese, shredded
- 2/3 cup whipped salad dressing
- ½ cup milk
- Salt, as required

Directions
1. In a large bowl, add all the ingredients and mix well.
2. Transfer the mixture into a baking pan and spread in an even layer.
3. Press "Power Button" of Air Fry Oven and turn the dial to select the "Air Bake" mode.
4. Press the Time button and again turn the dial to set the cooking time to 45 minutes.
5. Now push the Temp button and rotate the dial to set the temperature at 375 degrees F.
6. Press "Start/Pause" button to start.
7. When the unit beeps to show that it is preheated, open the lid.
8. Arrange pan over the "Wire Rack" and insert in the oven.
9. Serve hot.

CRISPY SAUSAGE BITES

Total Time: 20 minutes

Serves: 12

Ingredients
- Nonstick cooking spray
- 2 lbs. spicy pork sausage
- 1 ½ cups Bisquick
- 4 cups sharp cheddar cheese, grated
- ½ cup onion, diced fine
- 2 tsp pepper
- 2 tsp garlic, diced fine

Directions
1. Lightly spray baking pan with cooking spray.
2. In a large bowl, combine all ingredients. Form into 1-inch balls and place on baking pan, these will need to be cooked in batches.

3. Set oven to bake on 375°F for 20 minutes. After 5 minutes, place baking pan in position 2 and cook 12-15 minutes or until golden brown. Repeat with remaining sausage bites. Serve immediately.

PUFFEd ASPARAGUS SPEARS

Total Time: 30 minutes

Serves: 10

Ingredients
- Nonstick cooking spray
- 3 oz. prosciutto, sliced thin & cut in 30 long strips
- 30 asparagus spears, trimmed
- 10 (14 x 9-inch) sheets phyllo dough, thawed

Directions
1. Place baking pan in position 2 of the oven.
2. Wrap each asparagus spear with a piece of prosciutto, like a barber pole.
3. One at a time, place a sheet of phyllo on a work surface and cut into 3 4 1/2x9-inch rectangles.
4. Place an asparagus spear across a short end and roll up. Place in a single layer in the fryer basket. Spray with cooking spray.
5. Place the basket in the oven and set to air fry on 450°F for 10 minutes. Cook until phyllo is crisp and golden, about 8-10 minutes, turning over halfway through cooking time. Repeat with remaining ingredients. Serve warm.

WONTON POPPERS

Total Time: 25 minutes

Serves: 10

Ingredients
- Nonstick cooking spray
- 1 package refrigerated square wonton wrappers
- 1 8-ounce package cream cheese, softened
- 3 jalapenos, seeds and ribs removed, finely chopped
- 1/2 cup shredded cheddar cheese

Directions
1. Place baking pan in position 2 of the oven. Lightly spray fryer basket with cooking spray.
2. In a large bowl, combine all ingredients except the wrappers until combined.
3. Lay wrappers in a single layer on a baking sheet. Spoon a teaspoon of filling in the center. Moisten the edges with water and fold wrappers over filling, pinching edges to seal. Place in a single layer in the basket.
4. Place the basket in the oven and set to air fry on 375°F for 10 minutes. Cook until golden brown and crisp, turning over halfway through cooking time. Repeat with remaining ingredients. Serve immediately.

PARTY PULL APART

Total Time: 35 minutes

Serves: 10

Ingredients
- 5 cloves garlic
- 1/3 cup fresh parsley
- 2 tbsp. olive oil
- 4 oz. mozzarella cheese, sliced
- 3 tbsp. butter
- 1/8 tsp salt
- 1 loaf sour dough bread

Directions

1. Place the rack in position 1 of the oven.
2. In a food processor, add garlic, parsley, and oil and pulse until garlic is chopped fine.
3. Stack the mozzarella cheese and cut into 1-inch squares.
4. Heat the butter in a small saucepan over medium heat. Add the garlic mixture and salt and cook 2 minutes, stirring occasionally. Remove from heat.
5. Use a sharp, serrated knife to make 1-inch diagonal cuts across the bread being careful not to cut all the way through.
6. With a spoon, drizzle garlic butter into the cuts in the bread. Stack 3-4 cheese squares and place in each of the cuts.
7. Place the bread on a sheet of foil and fold up the sides. Cut a second piece of foil just big enough to cover the top.
8. Set oven to convection bake on 350°F for 25 minutes. After 5 minutes, place the bread in the oven and bake 10 minutes.
9. Remove the top piece of foil and bake 10 minutes more until the cheese has completely melted. Serve immediately.

EASY CHEESY STUFFEd MUSHROOMS

Prep time 25 minutes

Serves: 4

Ingredients
- Nonstick cooking spray
- 1/3 cup cream cheese, soft
- 1 tbsp. parmesan cheese, grated
- ¼ tsp garlic salt
- 2 tbsp. spinach, thaw, press dry & chop
- 8 oz. mushrooms, rinsed & stems removed
- 1 tbsp. panko bread crumbs

Directions
1. Lightly spray baking sheet with cooking spray.
2. In a medium bowl, combine cream cheese, parmesan, salt, and spinach, mix well.
3. Place mushrooms on baking sheet and fill with cheese mixture. Sprinkle bread crumbs over top.
4. Set oven to bake on 350°F for 20 minutes. After 5 minutes, place baking pan in position 2 of the oven and cook mushrooms 15 minutes until tops are lightly browned. Serve hot.

DESSERT RECIPES

QUICK COFFEE CAKE

Total Time: 30 minutes
Serves: 2
Ingredients
- ¼ cup butter
- ½ tsp instant coffee
- 1 tbsp black coffee, brewed
- 1 egg
- ¼ cup sugar
- ¼ cup flour
- 1 tsp cocoa powder
- Powdered sugar, for icing

Directions
1. Preheat Cuisinart on Bake function to 330 F. Beat the sugar and egg together in a bowl. Beat in cocoa, instant and black coffees; stir in flour. Transfer the batter to a greased cake pan. Cook for 15 minutes. Dust with powdered sugar and serve.

GLUTEN-FREE FRIEd BANANAS

Total Time: 15 minutes
Serves: 8
Ingredients
- 8 bananas
- 3 tbsp vegetable oil
- 3 tbsp cornflour
- 1 egg white
- ¾ cup breadcrumbs

Directions
1. Preheat Cuisinart on Toast function to 350 F. Combine the oil and breadcrumbs in a small bowl. Coat the bananas with the corn flour first, brush them with egg white, and dip them in the breadcrumb mixture. Arrange on a lined baking sheet and cook for 8-12 minutes. Serve.

VANILLA ALMOND COOKIES

Total Time: 45 minutes
Serves: 4
Ingredients
- 8 egg whites
- ½ tsp almond extract
- 1 ⅓ cups sugar
- 2 tsp lemon juice
- 1 ½ tsp vanilla extract
- Melted dark chocolate to drizzle

Directions
1. In a bowl, add egg whites and lemon juice. Beat using an electric mixer until foamy. Slowly add the sugar and continue beating until completely combined; stir in almond and vanilla extracts. Line the Air Fryer pan with parchment paper. Fill a piping bag with the meringue mixture and pipe as many mounds on the baking pan as you can leaving 2-inch spaces between each mound.
2. Cook at 350 F for 5 minutes on Bake function. Reduce the temperature to 320 F and bake for 15 more minutes. Then, reduce the heat to 190 F and cook for 15 minutes. Let cool for 2 hours. Drizzle with dark chocolate and serve.

LOBSTER TAILS WITH WHITE WINE SAUCE

Total Time: 24 minutes
Serves: 4
Ingredients
- lobster tails, shell cut from the top
- onion, quartered
- cup butter
- p wine
- honey
- 6 garlic cloves crushed
- 1 tablespoon lemon juice
- 1 teaspoon salt or to taste
- Cracked pepper to taste

DESSERT RECIPES

QUICK COFFEE CAKE

Total Time: 30 minutes
Serves: 2
Ingredients
- ¼ cup butter
- ½ tsp instant coffee
- 1 tbsp black coffee, brewed
- 1 egg
- ¼ cup sugar
- ¼ cup flour
- 1 tsp cocoa powder
- Powdered sugar, for icing

Directions
1. Preheat Cuisinart on Bake function to 330 F. Beat the sugar and egg together in a bowl. Beat in cocoa, instant and black coffees; stir in flour. Transfer the batter to a greased cake pan. Cook for 15 minutes. Dust with powdered sugar and serve.

GLUTEN-FREE FRIEd BANANAS

Total Time: 15 minutes
Serves: 8
Ingredients
- 8 bananas
- 3 tbsp vegetable oil
- 3 tbsp cornflour
- 1 egg white
- ¾ cup breadcrumbs

Directions
1. Preheat Cuisinart on Toast function to 350 F. Combine the oil and breadcrumbs in a small bowl. Coat the bananas with the corn flour first, brush them with egg white, and dip them in the breadcrumb mixture. Arrange on a lined baking sheet and cook for 8-12 minutes. Serve.

VANILLA ALMOND COOKIES

Total Time: 45 minutes
Serves: 4
Ingredients
- 8 egg whites
- ½ tsp almond extract
- 1 ⅓ cups sugar
- 2 tsp lemon juice
- 1 ½ tsp vanilla extract
- Melted dark chocolate to drizzle

Directions
1. In a bowl, add egg whites and lemon juice. Beat using an electric mixer until foamy. Slowly add the sugar and continue beating until completely combined; stir in almond and vanilla extracts. Line the Air Fryer pan with parchment paper. Fill a piping bag with the meringue mixture and pipe as many mounds on the baking pan as you can leaving 2-inch spaces between each mound.
2. Cook at 350 F for 5 minutes on Bake function. Reduce the temperature to 320 F and bake for 15 more minutes. Then, reduce the heat to 190 F and cook for 15 minutes. Let cool for 2 hours. Drizzle with dark chocolate and serve.

LOBSTER TAILS WITH WHITE WINE SAUCE

Total Time: 24 minutes
Serves: 4
Ingredients
- 4 lobster tails, shell cut from the top
- 1/2 onion, quartered
- 1/2 cup butter
- 1/3 cup wine
- 1/4 cup honey
- 6 garlic cloves crushed
- 1 tablespoon lemon juice
- 1 teaspoon salt or to taste
- Cracked pepper to taste

- Lemon slices to serve
- 2 tablespoons fresh chopped parsley

Directions
1. Place the lobster tails in the oven's baking tray.
2. Whisk rest of the ingredients in a bowl and pour over the lobster tails.
3. Press "Power Button" of Air Fry Oven and turn the dial to select the "Broil" mode.
4. Press the Time button and again turn the dial to set the cooking time to 14 minutes.
5. Now push the Temp button and rotate the dial to set the temperature at 350 degrees F.
6. Once preheated, place the lobster's baking tray in the oven and close its lid.
7. Serve warm.

BROILEd LOBSTER TAILS

Total Time: 16 minutes
Serves: 4
Ingredients
- 2 lobster tails, shell cut from the top
- 1/2 cup butter, melted
- 1/2 teaspoon ground paprika
- Salt to taste
- White pepper, to taste
- 1 lemon, juiced

Directions
1. Place the lobster tails in the oven's baking tray.
2. Whisk rest of the ingredients in a bowl and pour over the lobster tails.
3. Press "Power Button" of Air Fry Oven and turn the dial to select the "Broil" mode.
4. Press the Time button and again turn the dial to set the cooking time to 6 minutes.
5. Now push the Temp button and rotate the dial to set the temperature at 350 degrees F.
6. Once preheated, place the lobster's baking tray in the oven and close its lid.
7. Serve warm.

PAPRIKA LOBSTER TAIL

Total Time: 20 minutes
Serves: 4
Ingredients
- 2 (4 to 6 oz) Lobster Tails, shell cut from the top
- 1/8 teaspoon salt
- 1/8 teaspoon black pepper
- 1/8 teaspoon paprika
- 2 tablespoon butter
- 1/2 lemon, cut into wedges
- Chopped parsley for garnish

Directions
1. Place the lobster tails in the oven's baking tray.
2. Whisk rest of the ingredients in a bowl and pour over the lobster tails.
3. Press "Power Button" of Air Fry Oven and turn the dial to select the "Broil" mode.
4. Press the Time button and again turn the dial to set the cooking time to 10 minutes.
5. Now push the Temp button and rotate the dial to set the temperature at 350 degrees F.
6. Once preheated, place the lobster's baking tray in the oven and close its lid.
7. Serve warm.

LOBSTER TAILS WITH LEMON BUTTER

Total Time: 18 minutes
Serves: 4
Ingredients
- 4 lobster tails, shell cut from the top
- 1 tablespoon fresh parsley, chopped
- 2 garlic cloves, pressed
- 1 teaspoon Dijon mustard
- 1/4 teaspoon salt
- 1/8 teaspoon black pepper
- 1 1/2 tablespoon olive oil
- 1 1/2 tablespoon fresh lemon juice
- 4 tablespoon butter, divided

Directions
1. Place the lobster tails in the oven's baking tray.

2. Whisk rest of the ingredients in a bowl and pour over the lobster tails.
3. Press "Power Button" of Air Fry Oven and turn the dial to select the "Broil" mode.
4. Press the Time button and again turn the dial to set the cooking time to 8 minutes.
5. Now push the Temp button and rotate the dial to set the temperature at 350 degrees F.
6. Once preheated, place the lobster's baking tray in the oven and close its lid.
7. Serve warm.

SHEET PAN SEAFOOd BAKE

Total Time: 24 minutes
Serves: 4
Ingredients
- 2 corn ears, husked and diced
- 1 lb. red potatoes, boiled, diced
- 2 lbs. clams, scrubbed
- 1 lb. shrimp, peeled and de-veined
- 12 oz. sausage, sliced
- 1/2 red onion, sliced
- 4 lobster tails, peeled
- black pepper to taste
- 1 lemon, cut into wedges
- 1 cup butter
- 3 teaspoons minced garlic
- 1 tablespoon Old Bay seasoning
- fresh parsley for garnish

Directions
1. Toss all the veggies, corn, seafood, oil, and seasoning in a baking tray.
2. Press "Power Button" of Air Fry Oven and turn the dial to select the "Broil" mode.
3. Press the Time button and again turn the dial to set the cooking time to 14 minutes.
4. Now push the Temp button and rotate the dial to set the temperature at 425 degrees F.
5. Once preheated, place the seafood's baking tray in the oven and close its lid.
6. Serve warm.